REMINISCENCES

OF

WIGTONSHIRE

ISBN 1 872350 51 8

Published & Typeset by
G.C. Book Publishers Ltd
17 North Main Street
Wigtown
Scotland DG8 9HL
Tel/fax 01988 402499

Printed in Great Britain by The Cromwell Press
Broughton Gifford, Wiltshire

INTRODUCTION

Surviving eye-witness accounts of Wigtownshire before 1900 stem inevitably from the more educated population, most of whom had a formal grounding in the classics. One such was Andrew Symson, episcopalian minister of Kirkinner, who recorded events and conditions relating mainly to the middle and upper classes in his book, "A Large Description of Galloway" (1684). This work, unpublished in his lifetime, is one of the major sources of insight into life during the 17th century. Likewise, Peter Handy M'Kerlie, whose invaluable five volume work, entitled "Lands and their Owners in Galloway" (published over a period from 1872-1879) restricted his observations to the rise and fall of the great houses and their influence. No attempt was made by either author to present to the reader an insight into the conditions of the working classes.

There is no doubt that the social divide between the landed aristocracy and the common people caused the latter to be disregarded by the more privileged historian, while the lack of education available to would-be working class authors, and, what is more the lack of finance to meet publishing costs, formed fundamental obstacles to any authentic, written record of working class life. The final obstacle, to be negotiated by a working class author making an honest record was the probability of incurring the wrath of an employer or landlord, with the consequence of eviction or loss of employment. Accordingly any surviving document attempting to publicise authentic working class experience is to be welcomed as a significant historical source

A classic case of coercion by the influential in the community was the treatment of John MacNeillie on the publication of his book entitled "Wigtown Ploughman" published in 1939 and serialised in the "Sunday Mail". Although a young man at the time, in his early twenties, MacNeillie had an uncanny insight into the working conditions of the ordinary farm worker that prevailed at the beginning of this century. The book caused a furore, especially amongst the members of the Kirk who saw it as subversive and a distortion of the truth. John MacNeillie was forced by the influence of the minority to leave the area and in effect never to return. Needless to say he never let it destroy his creativity and after changing his pen name to the Gaelic version of his real name he became Ian Niall the successful writer with over 40 books to his credit, along with a regular column in "Country Life" entitled "Countryman's Notes".

Samuel Robinson, however was not over duly influenced by his so called 'betters'. Born in 1786 of farm-working parents, he attended the Parish school at Barglass. In 1800, he was given the opportunity to take up an apprenticeship on his uncle's ship the "Lady Neilson" which sailed from Liverpool as a slaver. He left the sea in 1804 at the age of eighteen after an injury to his ankle.

In 1867 he had published a booklet entitled "A Sailor Boy's Experiences". This publication records his four years at sea in the form of letters written home at the time. This, however, is simply the form of presentation that he has chosen to give the work an air of authenticity. It is obvious from the way that the letters are written that they could not be the work of a boy of fourteen. It would appear that he has used genuine letters written at the time and enhanced them from either his journals or his memory, or perhaps both.

This book was obviously a success as in 1872 he caused to be published yet another book, "Reminiscences in Wigtownshire". It was a record of his early days in Kirkinner in the Machars and Kirkcolm in the Rhinns. The vivid descriptions of life in Wigtownshire have been described by some as the most important eye-witness accounts recorded. It is therefore a great privilege to include this volume, in its entirety, in our "Local History Series".

Samuel Robinson died in Lesmahagow in 1874 at the age of 88.

REMINISCENCES

OF

WIGTONSHIRE

ABOUT THE CLOSE OF LAST CENTURY,

WITH CONTRASTS, AND

AN APPENDIX OF ODDS AND ENDS IN RHYME.

BY

SAMUEL ROBINSON,
AUTHOR OF "A SAILOR BOY'S EXPERIENCE.

"My son, fear thou the Lord, honour the King, and meddle not with those who are given to change." - Solomon.

HAMILTON:
PRINTED BY W. NAISMITH, 38 CADZOW STREET.
MDCCCLXXII.

"O Scotia! my dear, my native soil,
  For whom my warmest wish to heaven is sent!
Long may thy hardy sons of rustic toil
  Be blest with health, and peace, and sweet content!
And, O! may heaven their simple lives prevent
  From Luxury's contagion, weak and vile;
Then, howe'er crowns and coronets be rent,
  A virtuous populace may rise the while,
And stand a wall of fire around their much loved isle."

                                                    - Burns.

PREFACE.

THERE is a standing joke against the poor Scotchman that "if he gets in his wee finger, he will work in his hale haun." Perhaps I am about to subject myself to that charge, by once more thrusting my observations in life on the notice of my countrymen. But I do so under a hopeful impression that, as they patronised me far beyond my most sanguine hopes on my first attempt - "The Sailor Boy's Experience" - they will once more treat with charitable indulgence the second and last. It may naturally be asked why uneducated people presume to write and publish at all. For my own part, I truly say that, when I commenced to write "The Sailor Boy's Experience," it was merely for my own amusement, and with as little intention of publishing as I have at this moment of attempting to fly to the moon. The fact that it ever was published at all arose out of the following circumstances. A clerical gentleman with whom I was slightly acquainted - a gentleman of the highest talent and unbounded benevolence, a man on whom one cannot confer a higher favour than to ask him to oblige them - having learned something of what I was about, requested a sight of the manuscript, and at once pronounced it readable, and twelve hundred copies were soon in the hands of the public. On its appearance, another rev. gentleman in a distant part of the country, of equal talent, shortly reviewed the little book in an article in the Stranraer Free Press, from which

I beg to give an extract:- "This is a book of which it is not too much to say that it is a marvellous production for a man wholly self-educated. He possesses descriptive powers of a very high character, and what he sees he can convey with life-like truthfulness to the mind of his readers. On the whole we heartily recommend this little volume. It gives an interesting glimpse of a strange old world. It is a singular book to be written by a self-taught old man, and affords the assurance that, if he would give us a story or two about his early days in Wigtonshire, he would add a very readable chapter to the annals of Galloway. Let him try." Now it is singular that this was precisely the advice that my old adviser had previously given me, to "try again," and these "Reminiscences" are the result. Such is a part of the apology I have to offer for a second intrusion on public notice of portions of my experiences in the world; but whether I have succeeded in "adding a readable chapter to the annals" of my native county, as the rev. gentleman anticipated, and what I would have wished to do, must be left entirely to the judgement of the reader. I have added a few rhymes, about which I shall only say, that as I have nothing to say in their favour, I shall hold my tongue, as, no doubt, there will be enough of fault found, without my lending a hand to disparage them.

S.R.

PINE COTTAGE, LESMAHAGOW,
    January, 1872.

REMINISCENCES OF WIGTONSHIRE.

CHAPTER I.

THERE is something both pleasant and painful in the retrospect of a life of fourscore and four years. The youthful joys of the family circle, while under the watchful eyes of loving and careful parents, and schoolboy days, when kindred spirits attract one another, and lasting friendships are formed, in spite of little tiffs and short-lived fits of warmth of temper, are remembered with feelings of deep emotion. Entering the world on our own account, matters assume quite a different aspect. How many hard rubs and heartburnings are we subjected to - from the selfishness of one, the treachery of another, the cool, studied villainy of a third, and "the most unkindly cut of all" - the cooling of one whom we had formerly relied upon as a warm, devoted brother! Advancing in our onward course, our parents, brothers, sisters, and schoolfellows drop one by one into the narrow house -

"Wi' lowly roof o' sward sae green;"

or hie away to other lands in search of that wealth which it is impossible for sterile, old Caledonia to bestow on all her hardy sons. Many, in that search, lay down their bones early in life, from the pestilential nature of those sunny lands that "lured them to the tomb." Others, more fortunate, acquire wealth in abundance - doing so, however, at the price of much painful anxiety and a shattered constitution - wander home to die - frequently bequeathing their hard-earned money to those who shew little respect to the memory of those who toiled so hard in the acquisition of it. But it would not be fair to show only the gloomy side of the picture. There are white spots in it which counterbalance the dark ones. As generation after generation passes away, there are happy homes, fond endearments in early life producing happy unions, warm and lasting friendships, durable as life, like oases for refreshment for the traveller in desert-green spots with springs of pure water, surrounded with palm trees. However unwilling we may be to admit the fact, there are more of these white spots in the life of everybody than are duly appreciated - we are so prone to look at the dark side. And there is no doubt many apparent hardships are "blessings in disguise." Such is life!

I first opened my eyes in a very homely straw-roofed cottage, at a place called "The Signpost," on a very pleasant piece of tableland, on the farm of Balfern, parish of Kirkinner, Wigtonshire, on the 22d day of September, 1786. It stood - it stands no longer, the hare now crouches on the cold hearth - on the east side of the road between the ancient burghs of Wigton and Whithorn. At the place where the cottage stood, a road diverged, leading to the more modern hamlet of Garlieston. A signpost stood at the spot to direct the traveller; hence the name.

The history of the period is written, and it is well-known to have been a bloody and eventful one. The French Revolution was then running its infamous career, when deeds were done unsurpassed in atrocity in the history of any age or country. America had just gained her independence; a rebellion was brewing in Ireland - that unhappy country which no concession or indulgence can satisfy; and Great Britain was waging a fierce warfare with almost the whole continental powers. I would not have noted this (as a history of the time is not my intention) had it not been that events arose from the state of matters which caused much distress in Galloway, as well as in every other portion of the kingdom - events which I will have occasion often to allude to in this simple narrative of changes which have taken place in the county during the course of my long life. In order to make the early portion of my reminiscences more intelligible,

I must be indulged in the liberty of stepping back a few years, in order to trace the causes of many of the provocations and annoyances to which all classes were more or less subjected. Whether the war, which raged with so much fury, with short intervals, for about forty years, was a "just and necessary one," or not - I do not pretend to be a judge; although the clergymen every Sunday declared it to be so, when they implored a blessing on His Majesty's arms in the prosecution of it. No doubt the enemy claimed the same privilege - while it would be difficult to convince some people that it was just and necessary on both sides. But, whether just or unjust, the consequences were the same to those who provided muscles and sinews to carry it on. The heartburning and deep sorrow caused by the draining away, by enlistment, trepanning, and other means, of many husbands and sons leaving so many families destitute - caused a wailing in the county similar to that of the Egyptians when in every house the firstborn was found a corpse. The enormous amount of taxation necessary to carry on the war was very distressing, particularly on the labouring class, as everything they either ate or wore went up to starvation prices. Tea and sugar, which had formerly been considered luxuries, had now become necessaries of life almost with all classes. The former rose to eight shillings per pound; sugar, of very moderate quality, one shilling; soap, the same price; salt, that indispensable article, went up as high as four shillings and sixpence per seventeen and a-half pounds; wheat, from seventeen to twenty shillings per Winchester bushel; and other things in proportion. I recollect well, when scarcely able to perform the feat, often running along with my industrious mother to the seashore, where she went with cans to carry home salt water, which she boiled, and thereby obtained small quantities of salt. This, however, was a breach of the law, and had the exciseman been aware, he could have claimed a fine. I also recollect of going to the fields with her, flourishing an old hook, on pretence of assisting her in cutting and gathering into heaps, thistles, docks, and other rank weeds, which in those days were no scarce article. When dried they were burned, the ashes carefully collected, of which a lye was made, in which the family linen was boiled, and washed out with a small portion of soap; urine and Brazil soap being used for the woollen articles.

Another weighty grievance to which the lower orders in this locality, as in other districts, were subjected, was the cruel impressment of their friends at sea, and draining away of husbands and sons, by fair or foul means, for the land service, thereby entailing an amount of distress which never can be calculated. The impressment of seamen and trepanning of landsmen for the army was an arbitrary stretch of power for which nothing but the sheer necessity of the case could at all be pleaded in excuse. The trepanning was a piece of villainy, for which no apology could atone. It was perpetrated at fairs and other public assemblies, where young men ''most do congregate,'' by recruiting parties bedizened with gold and ribbons, like mountebanks, with pockets full of money, enlivened by the spirit-stirring drum and fife. Meantime, the sergeant harangued the gaping gulls with all manner of lies about the ease, honour, and glory of the soldier's life, plying all who would take it with any quantity of liquor, till

> ''First ae caper, syne anither,
> They tent their reason a'thegither.''

Many from the excitement of the moment took the liberal bounty offered; while, into the pockets of the unwary were slipped new or marked coin. All were hailed before a magistrate; those who took the bounty, tested; the trepanned party refusing were searched, and King's money being found in their possession, all were bundled off to head quarters.

Another method was resorted to by the Government, by proposing to organise a kind of ''army in mass.'' Orders were sent to the Established clergy to give a list of all whom they considered loyal, trustworthy, labouring men, who were assembled in the church on a given day, and on agreeing to attend occasional drill, and to be embodied in the event of an invasion, received their choice of a musket or a pike. I recollect of my father choosing a musket, but the design was not carried out.

My reasons for publishing these sheets arose in a great measure from the request of a number of partial friends who patronised me so very liberally on the publication of a narrative of my sailor life; and I candidly confess that the advice coincided with my own feelings - a desire which a few lines of Goldsmith's "Traveller" will express much better than I can:-

> "In all my wanderings round this world of care;
> In all my griefs - and God has given my share -
> I still had hopes my latest hours to crown.
> Amidst these humble bowers to lay me down;
> My anxious days to husband near the close,
> And keep life's flame from wasting by repose
> Around my evening fire a group to draw,
> And tell of all I felt, and all I saw;
> And as a hare whom hounds and horns pursue,
> Pants to the place from whence at first she flew,
> I still had hopes, my long vexation past,
> Here to return and die at home at last."

CHAPTER II

THE first incident which left an impression on my infant mind is, naturally, to be first recorded. It was of no common kind, and arose out of no common occurrence. It was no less than an invasion by the mighty sea, on whose surface I was destined a few years after to roam far and wide. Our family consisted of father, mother, two sisters, and myself. We had moved from the Signpost to a new house close upon the shore of the bay of Wigton, on the celebrated lowlands of Baldoon. The house was newly built from a plan by the famed Basil Lord Daer, to whom the estate at that time belonged, and who was making vast improvements on it. Being a first-class land-surveyor, he designed and watched over these improvements with much care, in his great anxiety, almost adding night to day, and Sunday to the week. The houses, like all his improvements, were of a superior class - well built, slated and plastered a very uncommon thing in those days of even farm-houses.

The houses consisted of a kitchen and room, between which, in the centre, stood a small bed-closet and large wooden press, and are to this day the best and most commodious cottages in the district. Shortly after taking possession, one night, the moon being at the full, when of course the tides are highest, and a heavy gale of wind blowing from the west-ward - which is well-known to drive a heavy body of water up the channel between Isle of Man and Borrowhead - was doing its usual work. About midnight, when the tide was at its highest point, my father was alarmed by an unusual commotion outside, and leaped out of bed, when, to his astonishment, he found himself up to the knees in water, and on wading to the window beheld the waves chasing one another up the road in front with white manes on them. Mother got sadly alarmed, roused us up, lapped us in blankets, and insisted on an immediate exodus to higher ground. My father, however, was aware from the hour that the tide was on the turn. We kept the bed till daylight, when we were removed till the house dried. Father made the best of his way into the house attached to the end of our one to see what sort of weather an old Irishman called Hugh Casey and his son Mondy were making, who had fled from the rebellion in Ireland. He found them sitting astride the baulks of the roof.* A very unwonted affair occurred about this time which drew the whole inhabitants for miles round to the sands about a mile from my father's house. The tide ebbs out of the Wigton Bay and leaves many square miles of sand dry at low water. The affair alluded to was the stranding of two large whales which ran themselves aground, and were left to perish by the receding tide. I recollect distinctly seeing the black monsters in the distance, but was too young to go to them. Mr Mure, a young gentleman of much energy, and much esteemed in the county, who was then assistant to Mr Jeffrey, factor for the Earl of Selkirk, who at that time held the superiority over the Baldoon estate, in consequence of his kinsman, Lord Daer having to fly his country for his Jacobite propensities - mustered men and horses, cut up the fish, and obtained a large quantity of excellent oil.

While recording scenes of infancy, I may be permitted to record a visitation from another element to which we were often subjected during the ensuing winter. My father had removed to the farm of Barnhills, in Kirkholm, Rhinns of Galloway, in the service of the late John Drew, Esq. The farm bordered on the

---

[* In the year 1868 a similar visitation took place, and much damage was done to the embankment and wheat crop in the locality; and I witnessed the devastation with much interest - a period of seventy-eight years having intervened.]

sea shore, but the houses stood on a rising ground of considerable elevation, admirably placed to receive the benefit of every
gale from every direction, more particularly of those north-west
storms that often sweep with such fury through between Ireland
and Argyleshire as through a tunnel. The wonder was that the
old fabric - the dwelling house - stood at all. Fortunately,
however, there was a most substantial barn on the premises
which many times during our sojourn in Barnhills proved a city
of refuge during the frequent visitations of old Boreas in all their
fury. No matter what hour of the night, whenever the old rafters
began to crack, our warm-hearted, loving mother leaped up,
shouting, "Rise, Willie; the weans 'ill be smoor'd" - no word
of herself; when we were roused up, lapped in blankets, and
ensconced among clean straw, where we were kept till the gale
spent itself. Mr Drew having removed to another farm, my
father also went with him. The farm was in a very rough,
uncultivated condition, large portions of it covered with furze
of extraordinary dimensions, the extent of which it is scarcely
safe to give in the present day. It is a fact, however, that they
were quite high enough to shelter cattle or horses, which made
pass-ways through the patches, and sheltered in them from their
enemy, the cleg, in summer, and from the cold in winter - healthy
golden-crowned fellows on whom the patriarchs of the locality
could mark no visible change during their pilgrimage. The
breaking up of such land was no joke; vigorous measures,
however, were resorted to, and I remember my father ploughing
on the farm with a ponderous wooden machine, drawn by two
bullocks next the plough and two horses in traces, with a stout
young fellow as gadsman. It was customary in those days that
the regular soldiers were allowed to work for the farmers a
certain part of their time, and an old Highlander and his son were
employed forming drains, and their perseverance was astonishing. No matter how hard it blew or rained - be the weather hot

or cold - there they were from dark to dark plodding away. They wore kilts, which in cold, rainy weather was a very comfortless garment.

About this time an alarming incident took place which made a deep impression on my memory. The village of Newton stands close by Fineview, on the north-west corner of Lochryan, not far from our farm. Half-way between those places a bridge crosses a small stream, beside which stands a smith's shop - the smith's name being Cubbin: a most respectable man. A son of the family named Andrew, a fine active young man about eighteen years of age, was house-servant with Mr Drew, and was sent an errand one day to the village. I was then a very little fellow, and a favourite with poor Andrew, who took me by the hand to go with him to the clachan. When passing his father's house, as was very natural, he looked in for a few minutes. On passing the bridge, there is a considerable rise in the road. To make up for the time he stopped, he commenced to run as fast as I could keep up, holding me still by the hand, when instantly, standing up, a stream of blood burst out of his mouth - and he fell dead! I cannot tell how I felt; but I, naturally, ran back and gave the alarm, when poor Andrew was carried in, a corpse, to his mother - whom he had only, a few minutes before, left a stout, active, living son.

CHAPTER III.

DURING part of my school-boy days it was my good fortune to be domiciled with my grandparents - by the mother's side - Alexander Cowan, and Elspath M'Dowal, whom I will revere while memory lasts. Grandfather was one of the most diffident, unassuming men I ever met; a sound Presbyterian of the old Evangelical Cameronian school of the mildest type, without ostentation or hypocrisy. I stopped with them to be near the Parish School of Barglass.

I believe that a picture of the miserable hovel, called the Parish School, where I obtained the small portion of tuition, which fell to my share at Barglass, will represent, in a general way, the most of the country school-houses in the west of Scotland at the time of 1790. The walls were of the rudest kind of rubble work - it would never do to call it mason work - say thirty feet in length by fifteen wide, and perhaps eight high; one small window in each gable, eighteen inches square; one small door on the roadside - no window; two windows in back wall, east side, two feet six by one foot eight inches; roofed with oak poles, stript of the bark, which glittered like polished ebony from the smoke of many years, and thatched with straw; a "lum," right in the centre of the roof, of large dimensions, also of straw; the surface dug off the floor, raked tolerably smooth, and you have the school-room. A round spot in the centre of the floor, right under the "lum," was paved with small stones for the fire-place in winter, beside which stood a small round table and an arm-chair, upon which sat the good, kind-hearted old teacher, Mr John M'Millan, in all his glory. He was not a man of high talent nor much scholarship, but what he had was of sterling quality, and he meant well. There were three writing desks with benches to suit, of foreign timber, at one end of the room; the seats for the other classes were of a very homely character. They were old oak trees which had been dug out of the mosses of the neighbourhood, nearly as when they were found, as far as polishing was concerned, and propped up to suit the length of the lower limbs of his majesty's young subjects, the props being rough blocks of stone, or earthen sods. There was no use for hooks to hang cloaks upon, as there were no cloaks to hang. The teacher's house consisted of a ''but'' and a ''ben,'' and altogether superior to the school-room though still a very uncomfortable cabin. Early in the present century the good old teacher and the old wigwam died together. A small, comfortable school-room was built close by the site of the old one, which has since been superseded by buildings beside the church, more in accordance with the spirit of the times - comfortable palaces, when contrasted with that which I have attempted to describe. Before proceeding further in describing the means and usage's of my time, in contrast with the very superior system of the present day, I would beg to be allowed to borrow a few more lines from Goldsmith, as an epitaph on the venerable old teacher and the well remembered old house.

> ''Beside yon straggling fence, that skirts the way
> With blossom'd furze, unprofitably gay;
> There, in his noisy mansion, skill'd to rule,
> The village master taught his little school -
> A man severe he was, and stern to view.
> I knew him well, and every truant knew:
> Well had the boding tremblers learnt to trace
> The day's disasters in his morning face:
> Full well they laughed with counterfeited glee
> At all his jokes - for many a joke had he:
> Full well the busy whisper circling round
> Convey'd the dismal tidings, when he frown'd.

Yet, he was kind, and if severe in aught,
The love he bore to learning was in fault.

* * * * * * * * * * * * * * *
But past is all his fame. The very spot,
Where many times he triumph'd, nigh forgot.''

As the immense advantage the scholars of the present day possess over those of a century ago is one of the subjects to which I wished to call general attention in my Reminiscences I will endeavour to contrast the state of the case at the different periods as impartially as I can.

The houses and teachers of bygone days I have attempted to sketch, and I am convinced it will suit a considerable portion of the men and houses of the time. Talented men and comfortable houses, no doubt, always existed in Scotland; but I know they were in the minority in Wigtonshire in the fag end of the 18th century. Setting aside the teacher altogether for the present, the advantage in the quality of the elementary books in favour of the present time over the other is incalculable. The class books of the Barglass schoolboy were in rotation as follows. The Shorter Catechism, Solomon's Proverbs, in pamphlet form, Reading made Easy, Old and New Testament, Barrie's or Mason's Collection, for advanced readers, and Dilworth's System of Arithmetic - but a pair of globes, a map or black board, would have frightened the Barglassians out of the old house. The mode of reading too (but especially the pronunciation of the letters of the alphabet), was of a very old-world type, and the usages of the school vulgar and unpolished. It is obvious that there was no use for a satchel in those days. The Collection and Catechism were thrust inside of the waistcoat, as he knew that one or more questions must be answered when he entered the school in the morning, and a psalm every Monday. I must be pardoned; in fact, I ought to receive thanks, for quoting

Blair's beautiful lines on "The Schoolboy in the Churchyard":-

"Oft in the lone churchyard, at night, I've seen,
By glimpse of moonshine chequering through the trees,
The schoolboy, with his satchel in his hand,
Whistling aloud, to keep his courage up,
And lightly tripping o'er the long, flat stones,
With nettles skirted and with moss o'ergrown,
That tell, in homely phrase, who lie below.
Sudden he starts, and hears, or thinks he hears,
The sound of something purring at his heels.
Full fast he flies, and dares not look behind,
Till out of breath he overtakes his fellows,
Who gather round, and wonder at the tale
Of horrid apparition, tall and ghastly,
That walks at dead of night, or takes his stand
O'er some new-opened grave - and, strange to tell,
Evanishes at crowing of the cock."

But though the Barglassian had no satchel, there was one indespensable appendage he must carry to school every winter morning a turf peat; if he omitted to do so he would be jostled from the great fire which was kept blazing in the middle of the floor the whole day. A strict watch was kept by the early comers on all as they entered in the morning, and if any one came in without the peat, a chorus of many voices would be heard shouting, "Maister, he hisna a peat."

Before taking leave of the old school, I must be permitted to give a correct account of a remarkable occurrence, - the last scene of a tragic character which the good old teacher led the. scholars, of whom I was one, to the churchyard to witness. The affair arose out of this true tale. The discontented spirit which has smouldered in Ireland ever since Popery has had the ascendancy in that unhappy country, and which was stimulated by the success of the American Rebellion and French Revolution, and was crushed out in the year 1798, was, at the time I speak of, in full feather. Early in the Nineties, great numbers of those scamps - croppies, as they were called, as cropped heads was a mark of being united, - not seeing any chance of immediate plunder at home, fled into Wigtonshire; others of a higher grade, but who had not a sufficient amount of patriotism, nor a deep enough sense of the woes of Ireland to induce them to stay at home and have a chance of a leaden bullet in their victualling office, or a swing at the end of six feet of a rope, also came over. The actors in the tragic tale spoken of were three of these fugitives, of the first class, - two brothers of the name of David and Joseph Crobbin and a cunning villain of the name of Daniel Hawkins. They all resided in David's house, who was married to a relation of the old schoolmaster, and resided on the farm of Bing, in Kirkinner parish. It was customary in those days for all the athletic youths of the district to assemble in the spring and summer evenings and amuse themselves at a game called "long bowls". The game was a noble one, and brought out the physical powers of a man without any damage. There were two three pound cannon balls, two parties of equal numbers opposed each other, and each individual, in succession, hurled the ball along the public road, and the party who arrived at the goal (perhaps a mile distant) by the "fewest number of the throws" was the victor.

That noble, healthful game has many years ago, with many other harmless and healthful amusements of the time, gone to the grave of all the Capulets; and many youths of the present day have found a more congenial way of passing their evenings by retiring to the whisky shop to enjoy their pipe or cigar.

But to my tale. It was a lovely evening in June, the writer, then a very little fellow, witnessing the whole affair. The three heroes of the tale were onlookers for a few minutes that evening and left early. Next morning the whole village was in an uproar on beholding the three Croppies marching handcuffed in charge of a posse of Sheriff-officers toward Wigton Jail. The whole affair soon came out - it was this, a sister of the Crobbins had been in service shortly before in the farm of Corwar, in the parish of Minnigaff, about fifteen miles from Kirkinner, and perhaps might have given them information of the whereabouts of things on the premises. Be that as it may, I saw them leaving the village about five in the evening on their way as it afterwards proved, to commit the robbery.

The time occupied in travelling thirty miles, returning laden with spoils, is almost incredible; yet there is nothing more true than that they accomplished the whole business in thirteen hours. To prevent the possibility of pursuit, the thieves bound the honest folks with ropes - securely as they thought. Fortunately, however, one young man managed to cast himself loose, and with great courage - for it was a dangerous business - managed to keep them in sight the whole way. To shun Newton-Stewart, the rogues crossed the river Cree at Machermore, the young man dodging them at a warey distance, which must have required much pluck and caution, at the time of year - when daylight is never away. He managed, however, to trace them to their own house, after stowing away a portion of the stuff in a clump of furze, half-a-mile from home. He returned to Wigton, a distance of four miles; got a band of officers, and came in on the gentlemen when at a hearty breakfast of mutton ham - part of the spoil. They were put in Wigton Jail; David in an arched cell, he being considered the projector of the raid; the other two in one room upstairs. Hawkins and Joseph managed to break out, the former getting clear off, while poor, simple Joe was caught stalking in a field of wheat, not having sense enough to lie down. They were tried at Dumfries Circuit, and condemned to die. This is the first act of the tragedy, but the Judge, perhaps to make a deeper impression in the locality in which they had lived, decreed that their corpses should be returned to Kirkinner, and that their coffins were to be opened and the bodies exposed to any who desired it. On the day when the coffins were expected, the old master sent me to the top of a lovely green hill which stands between the churchyard and where the old school-room stood, with orders to keep a sharp outlook on the road at Moorpark house, and on the first view of the cart I was to come and give the alarm. A few minutes only elapsed, after observing the cart, till the whole scholars, with the old gentleman at our head, were in full march for the churchyard. David's coffin was shut before we got there; but there lay a sight, that, should I live for a thousand years, and could retain my memory, I could not forget. There lay all that was mortal of poor Joe Crobbin, whose kind smile had often shone on me - another Abel slain by the deed of a guilty brother - who, every one knew well, was as innocent as a child of a wilful intention of committing the deed for which he suffered, and that it was forced upon him. There he lay with the rope round his neck, cut so as to reach the foot of the coffin, with the tallow with which the executioner had greased the rope, shining white in the hollow of the strands. The coffins must have been of a very strong order as the graves never subsided; and, a few weeks ago, at an interval of seventy-six years, I stood on the Crobbins' grave.

Much has been spoken and written on both sides of the question regarding capital punishments, a great many in the present age ignoring them as sanguinary and unwarrantable. This is surely a one-sided view of the matter. The celebrated Dr. Franklin seems to me to treat the matter with much fairness and common sense. He contrasts the different views taken by the English and American legislators on the subject, and justly blames the English law as unjust in hanging all thieves; while the Americans proportion punishment to crime. He also justly blames Butler, an English judge, for an unfair summing up, while condemning a man for stealing a horse. The judge said "You are not only to be hanged for stealing a horse, but that horses may not be stolen" - meaning, of course, that part of his punishment was to be inflicted for an example to others. Now, Franklin sensibly looks on this as cruel and unfair to the last degree. "Punish a man," he says, "to the full extent of the offence, but no farther." And he affirms "that no man has a right to be punished for an example to others," and calls it "unjust in any case to take away life for theft." It is a matter to be thankful for, that the principle is now admitted in English law, which is lately much humanised. But, between the punishment due for the violation of the law respecting property and the crime of murder, there is a great gulf fixed, which cannot and ought not to be bridged over. I have no right, nor have I any wish, to say one word regarding the apparent sanguinary spirit of the Mosaic law with respect to minor offences; but there is not a command in the five books which Moses wrote under Divine inspiration (let it be marked) so often reiterated as that in every case the wilful murderer should surely be put to death; "Whosoever sheddeth man's blood, by man shall his blood be shed" - is imperative in every case. It is quite true that there is something very repulsive in the idea of depriving a fellow-creature of that which we cannot give; and, for myself, had I the power to save his life - although convinced of his guilt - were he placed face to face with me to beg me to let him live, I know well I could not refuse to grant it; but, in so doing, I would be quite wrong. Be just before you are generous - is sound sentiment. There is a sickly sentimentalism on that subject in the present day largely indulged in, but no amount of such a spirit can cancel a divine command. Many of those benevolent individuals, convinced that a sentence of penal servitude is a more severe and repulsive one than immediate death, would advise its adoption. Allowing this to be true, where is their philanthropy when they insist on subjecting the victim to a mode of punishment which they themselves admit to be the more cruel and oppressive of the two. There is very little consistency in this.

In connection with the melancholy tale of those unfortunate men, I may perhaps be excused in giving a sketch of another fugitive from the Emerald Isle for the same cause; but a man of quite a different character.

His name was John Lauderdale, who, about the same time as the Crobbins, squatted in an old barn not far from their house. He was a middle-aged labouring nan, with a wife, three sons, and a daughter. He was of very unsteady habits, so much so as to avail himself of every chance of getting into a grog shop - drink deeply, and roar Croppie songs at the highest pitch of a very powerful but very unmusical voice, as long as luck, cash, or credit stood his friend, or his tongue and eyelids would wag. He had joined the Croppies early, and, finding out his mistake, took French leave of "ould Ireland," and sat down as aforesaid. He was an honest, cheerful, and agreeable person, and, when sober, a pleasant companion; possessed a fair portion of natural shrewdness and observing powers - particularly in finding out the weak point in the character of his associates. But he was more - he was a fair country rhymer, and actually published in Edinburgh a small volume of poems by subscription, which was fairly patronised a very uncommon circumstance in those days. As was to be expected from the temperament of the man, his poems were all of a light satirical cast, with nothing like sentiment or pathos, and outrageously personal. I knew him well, and, before I go farther, must be permitted to give a startling anecdote connected with his drinking habits. When very young, I, as I have already stated, stopped with my grandmother, who held a license for selling spirits, the only one in the village. I slept in a small closet off the kitchen, which was old Lauderdale's howf for at least three nights in the week, and when he got elevated, and commenced to shout, it made me tremble as if it had been the roar of a lion.

In a fit of remorse he made a vow that he would not drink a glass of spirits *in a public house* for a certain time, but he still hovered about, and by and by ventured in to enjoy the gossip. Luckily for him the closet window opened by a latch, and, when the glass was passing, I have seen him go outside, and, round to the window, bolt the whisky, which was handed out, and return to his place.

His book is lost. The late Ramsay M'Culloch, when collecting some legendary lore in the county, offered a handsome sum for a copy without success. His sons went to America, and, when John and Mary were well up in year, money came to take them to join their sons, which they at once did. The ruling spirit was still so strong in the old Croppie, that, on passing through Wigton on his way to the land of freedom, as he styled it, after priming well with *potheen*, he took his stand at the cross, and roared out, with all the power of his lungs, a favourite Croppie song of the day, the chorus of which was -

> "Viva la the new convention,
> Viva la republican,
> Viva la America,
> It was in you it first began."

In those days this was an indictable offence, but the magistrates wisely made a joke of it. One parting word with my good old friend Mary Conchie, his wife, must be allowed me. By what freak of nature they came together it would be vain to enquire, for they were as opposite in their nature and habits as could be imagined. She was one of the most quiet, timid, simple little women that ever lived; and, to do justice to old John, he knew her value, and in all his recklessness, drunk or sober, invariably treated her with kindness. I have seen him, when she presented her little round good-humoured face, on coming to assist him home from his debauch, taking her on his knee, and dandling her like a baby, exclaim - "Never fear, by jing, I'll support you, Conchie." Like all Irish women, Mary had a taste for business, and from the imperfect state of the agriculture of the period, numberless swamps swarming with leeches were at hand. Of these she availed herself, and sold extensively. She also established a trade in chickens, eggs, &c., with all the respectable houses in town and country, thereby managing to make old John comfortable at home, and even enabling him to indulge his convivial propensities oftener than he otherwise could have done. Peace to their memories! But this is a digression.

CHAPTER IV.

A most salutary change is very obvious in the highly improved physical appearance of the Gallovedians, in the course of the nineteenth century, arising from the improved nature of the cleansing stuffs for the use of the laundry and personal cleanliness; but par excellence - from the superior quality of the food of the working portion of the community. The slow but steady progress in this refining process of the human system in this county does not seem to have claimed the amount of public attention which it is entitled to; although the beneficial effects are very obvious and very gratifying. It is well known that the staple commodity of human food for the major part of the inhabitants of Scotland in bygone ages, was oatmeal; and, although the nutritive quality of this article is of a high standard, it is as well known, that its heating quality and gross influence on the blood, when largely indulged in, is beyond all contradiction. Let it also be noted, that any one who has, even superficially watched the movement of things generally, knows that, till within comparatively a few years back, no such thing as fresh butcher meat was ever calculated upon above a few days in the course of the year, when the annual meat was provided and salted up. Even potatoes, which, like all other vegetables, have a tendency to cool and purify the blood, were generally eaten with herrings which had lain in pickle no man could tell how long, which neutralized their good effects. It was so with all other vegetables, they were cooked along with a mass of meat that had perhaps floated in brine for many months, and, not unlikely, hung in the smoky kitchen as long. In fact, with the exception of a little fresh butter, an egg, and a cup of tea twice a week, with the everlasting oatcake, scarcely anything fresh was ever tasted. What sort of blood was likely to be formed out of such inflammable materials as these! Many families contented themselves with the carcase of a pig, which the industry of the careful wife had nursed throughout the year, and salted up at Martinmas, one of the hams being hung up in the smoke until turf-cutting time, for the peaters' dinner, where it was served up as yellow as a honeycomb. There was indeed a certain portion of milk and vegetables forthcoming, but not in proportion to the scorbutic element, and quite inadequate to counteract their effects. But that remarkable agent for cleansing the blood and refining the human frame - wheaten flour - was not unknown in the county; yet if tasted at all by the labouring portion of the people, it was only as a great luxury. In the event of a funeral, a marriage, or baptism, a small quantity was got, - but intimation had to be given to the baker what quantity would be required, some days before it was needed. When I was old enough to be capable to be trusted to go on a message to Whithorn or Wigton, a distance of, say seven miles, one old woman in each royal burgh was the sole public baker old Flora Hannah in the former, and Jenny Sloan in the latter. If fortunate enough to have "one splendid penny" of my own, I often hesitated, on seeing the tempting morsel withering in the window, where it had probably lain for a week, whether I would make myself happy with the rare bit of bread, exactly the shape and size of a middle-sized cucumber, or a new ballad, of which I was even then gathering a collection.

What an amazing revolution in this matter have a few years brought about! Fancy two old women supplying two thirds of a county with wheaten bread! whilst now we have a baker or two in almost every village. Take, for example, a village containing fifteen or sixteen hundred inhabitants, where I have resided for some time. In this hamlet there are four baking establishments, vans running daily, besides considerable quantities imported from other towns. It is, in fact, become the staple commodity of Scotland's food, and well that it is so.

Other agents, too, in this renovating process must have their need of praise. The all but universal use of fresh butcher meat, with the improved quality, and enlarged use of vegetables, and that remarkable nutritive agent - sugar, have also all had a corresponding influence in producing that delightful change in tle plysical improvement of the whole community, which no one who has lived as long as I have done, can fail in observing. Not only has the improved quality of the food, and external appliances, purified the blood and polished the external surface of the body - the very figure of the person, and features of the face, have improved to a very visible extent. Indeed, the process is visibly progressing as the personal appearance of the majority in every generation seems to be an improvement on the past. This is perhaps most visible in children, and particularly in females. This is very pleasant to look upon by every one, more so by one who can look back on three-fourths of a century, and remember having seen the thin hair of almost every third child he met a filthy clotted mass, from disease of the blood; while the wrists and fingers were very unpleasant. What a contrast now! The pure skin and rosy faces of the little ones - without an exception - with hair as light as thistle down, floating about their ears, with even refined features, make the beholder's heart rejoice. A very notable change is visible in the improved quality and getting up of the wearing apparel - the ladies, as in all improvements, taking the lead, - an exceptional bundle of bow and hair on the back of the head, not to be included in the improvements.

Much of the obvious refinement during late years is, no doubt, due to the elementary books now, more or less, in every family, treating, as they do, of everything connected with life and manners, as well as art and science. These must have had much to do with the refining process which has been going on and is still in progress. A great deal of the means of preserving the beauty of the "human face divine" from deformity, is due to Dr Jenner's noble art of vaccination, for the prevention of natural smallpox. Before his time, every visitation of that loathsome disease (and they were frequent), carried off its victims in thousands, and those who escaped with life were sadly disfigured. The proof of the efficacy of vaccination lies in the fact that the malady may almost be said to have been conquered. Even when it does pay an occasional visit, in ninety-nine cases out of a hundred, the victim has never been cut ; while scarcely is, an individual we meet, under fifty years of age, seen bearing the unseemly mark of the old enemy.

I have spoken of the great advantages enjoyed by the people of the present day over those of a century ago, in respect of personal comfort from the cheap and much improved quality of cleansing materials, and the equally improved quality of the food of the million, and I now beg the reader to have a little patience with me while I say a few words on the very uncomfortable condition of the agricultural portion of the natives in bygone times, and, by way of accounting for the indifference the farmers displayed regarding the hovels of their married servants, I will give a literal description of the first farm-house I served in, and there were many to which the sketch would apply. The house referred to was connected with a farm of four hundred acres; it stood or rather leant against a piece of rising ground from which the surface was dug away, and the floor underwent no further preparation, so that the one end of the erection stood perhaps six feet higher than the other - that is to say, they just built on the incline as they found it. The first process in the erection was performed by the carpenter. A lot of oak trees of different diameters which had been dug out of moss bogs in the locality were provided, and the roof bound by boring auger holes in the different pieces, and bolting them together with oak trennels of inch and half in diameter, leaving the projecting ends, no matter how long uncut off. Eight uprights, of eight feet in length, were cut out of the strongest trees, and set on end at the proper distances on each side on which to rest the couples, four in number on a house of fifty feet in length, and firmly secured. The end of each couple, when set on the upright, was bolted to it with trennels through a coupling piece of wood, which made all firm, while strong poles were laid along the couples horizontally, and others of a lighter description from eave to roof-tree, to which the thatch was to be sewed by plaited ropes of straw. This was all done (except the thatch), before the mason was thought of. The stones were gathered promiscuously, a little mortar of lime, or oftener soil, and the mason proceeded by building two thick gables, with a flue in one of them, and filling up the spaces between the uprights, and the house was finished. No plasterer or joiner was needed in what is called finishing, but a huge lum of bramble and straw was stuck up to do duty in the kitchen end, and a small chimney in the other the ridge having the same incline as the floor. But rough and uncouth as tlis structure seemed, when the floor was swept up and a bright fire blazing on the ground, there was a show of rude homely comfort about it beyond what could be expected; and, notwithstanding its rude construction, it stood firm at the time of my sojourn, though it must have battled with the war of elements for at least one hundred years.

Immediately in front, at right angles with the house, at a sufficient distance to allow a carriage to pass, stood a small house called the Chammer, a kind of lumber-room, in which was a bed for the two in-door male servants.

When the honest farmer was content with a fabric like this, it was not to be expected that his cottar was to have anything superior or even equal; and so it was. The cothouses were detached, in spots best suited for the surveillance of the farm; and many of them, although mean of themselves, stood in very cozy places and pleasant "feathery neuks."

With the exception of the roof the cottage was a facsimile of the other, but of more limited dimensions. It might be twenty-five feet by fifteen, in which space were sheltered the hind and family and in very many cases - the cow and poultry; while the pig - the only gentleman of the family - had a bedroom outside, but ate his meals in the kitchen, while the poultry dined on the crumbs he left. The value of a cow to a poor man who could purchase one was immense, and she was well worth her room. One-third of the cottage was allotted for her use, she going in and out of the same door as the family, often with the youngest child seated on her back steadied by another.

Indispensable articles of furniture in a peasant's house were two wooden beds, six feet by four, and as close and air-tight as they could be made; and when the sliding doors in front which did the duty of curtains, were shut, the inmates were as effectually closed up from the rest of the world as if in their coffins. Indeed, the prejudice against the admission of fresh air into dwelling houses in those days was astonishing, especially in times of sickness, when it was most essential to have it, and more particularly in cases of fever and smallpox, when life almost depended on free ventilation. Every crevice was carefully shut up, lest "a waff o' cauld air" should reach the patient, while groaning under a load of blankets sufficient to smother him, and when a mouthful of pure air was of more value than all the drugs in the world. And, to crown this absurd folly, the sick room was often crowded with well-meaning, though ill-advised, sympa-thising friends, disturbing the reflections of the patient, and assisting in poisoning the oft-respired atmosphere, which the most healthy of them found oppressive, often carrying away and spreading the disease.

In the cottar's cabin two of these wooden machines were placed end to end across the house, forming a partition to keep the cow to her own quarters, and leaving for her a passage on one side.

The poultry were perched above the cow. The cock, indeed, was a very useful member of the establishment, acting as timekeeper - clocks and watches not being so common as they have since become, the cock was the substitute. In the morning he was never asleep when his master should be awake, and by his rousing crow at the proper time paid well for his perch.

Perhaps I may be indulged in giving an anecdote of a similar kind told me by a native of that far-famed Scottish Arcadia, that land of battle and song, Ettrick Forest, where the cottage I have sketched in all its homeliness. They had no timepieces and it seems they left the regulation of the time to the natural habits of the cow instead of the cock, at least in the winter evenings. During the day, when the sun shone out, the shadow of a rock, a tree, or the cheering sunbeam on a certain point on the floor, through their little window, was quite reliable as indicating the proper time to put the dinner pot on the fire; but, in the dreary winter evenings, the cow, who stood behind the bed, gave the warning to put the supper pot on, which the watchful guidwife always did, 'when the cow shed her water the *second time*.'

It is very obvious that the housekeepers of those days felt the task of keeping such hovels clean and anything like comfortable, a very hopeless one, although many praiseworthy attempts were made to do so.

Let it never be doubted, however, that, in those lowly cabins, there existed, to a very great extent, as much true happiness and rational enjoyment, simple as it might be, as was ever to be met with in the most gaudy palaces of any age or nation.

And the crowning act of every evening, in a great number of those lowly homes, was the united petition of the parents:-

"That He, who stills the raven's clamorous nest,
And decks the lily fair in flowery pride,
Would, in the way His wisdom sees the best,
For them and for their little ones provide;
But chiefly in their hearts with grace divine preside."

The question may naturally be asked, If so much comfort and social happiness was attainable in such wigwams, why desire a change? Simply for this reason, that the good old uses, which alone made the old house a happy home, would lose none of their value by being transferred into more wholesome and more comfortable residences, and the real comfort of the individuals be every way promoted. It is quite unnecessary to describe the class of buildings of the present day that have superseded those I have here attempted to describe, as any one who reads my description, and looks round him, may judge for himself. But were my opinion of any weight in the matter, I would say that, in respect of house accommodation, in country districts particularly, it is one of the things that has not kept pace with many other improvements in Wigtonshire, as the face of the county is yet disgraced by huts in which many poor families are obliged to shelter, that are almost unfit for a hog of any taste; and much has yet to be done in replacing them with something more in unison with the advanced state of general refinement of the county.

CHAPTER V.

THE education question is doubtless that which claims the chief attention of every one; and, as I have endeavoured as simply, but as fairly as I could, to give the state of the matter in my time with scholars of my class, I could wish to be heard on the matter a little farther. The superior house accommodation has been noticed already, and need not be repeated. I also alluded to the very great disparity in the number and quality of the elementary books in the different periods, and the consequent advantage enjoyed by the scholar of later times in that respect. I said before that no satchel was needed in those days of turf and ''reading-made-easy,'' but now every school-boy one meets is groaning under a weary load, as large as a soldier's knapsack, choke-full of the condensed knowledge of every age and nation, while he also has the benefit of a comfortable room to study in, and a well qualified teacher to assist him in stowing away in his memory so rich a cargo.

The poet says -

> "Tis education forms the common mind,
> Just as the twig is bent the tree's inclined."

There is, no doubt, much truth in this; and, if so, surely it is not unreasonable to expect a corresponding amount of benefit to himself and society in accordance with his higher privileges; and that he will rise higher, and continue longer on the wing than the man of the straw hovel and turf-smoke. At the same time it would be satisfactory to know what portion of that immense wallet was secular, and what moral and religious, or if there was such a thing at all as a Bible. Our fathers considered the Bible an indispensable school-book; believing it to be the fountain of all true knowledge; consequently, it ought to be the foundation of all knowledge.

It seems, however, - if we are to believe the immaculate reformers of modern days, - that our fathers were quite mistaken about the nature and quality of the Book, and that it might safely be dispensed with in the school; and, as it had a tendency to corrupt the minds of Popish scholars and others of a similar creed, it would be quite unfair to allow it to enter a school. Few will deny that a well-educated rogue is more dangerous than an ignorant one, as his superior training puts it into his power to carry out his fraudulent plans much better than the other.

And this sentiment derives support from the alarming extent to which fraud and embezzlement, in every form, have been in operation so long by numbers of men who have had first-class education in the secular department.

No one who has watched the progress of events for some time can have failed to notice the working of this villainous propensity, from knights down to errand boys; and scarce a newspaper one takes in hand but tells of some defaulter in this way. No doubt the evil always existed; but it is obvious to the most superficial observer that the present fearful length it has come to arose simultaneously with the ejection of the moral and religious element from so many of the schools, making it evident that the one was the principal cause of the other.

The gradual increase of newspaper information is another means which must have done much to enlarge the views of all classes for a long time back: greatly beyond what was possible in my early life. No doubt the enormous price of all the elements of information - books, paper, postage, &c. - tended to retard the work of intellectual training. In the case of newspapers, I distinctly remember when a very young boy - the French

Revolution then running its bloody career, and all the ruling Powers in the civilised world struggling in deadly combat, and, as was natural, when every one was feverishly anxious for intelligence - that six London newspapers once a week were all that were received in the whole parish of Kirkinner. And I also remember my uncle, who was manager for one of the gentlemen who received one of them, used to read the news on a certain evening weekly to the inhabitants of the village, who met at his garden stile - hence called the Parliament stile. There is little doubt that the whole county was similarly situated.

All extremes are to be avoided as much as possible, as they all are dangerous. The papers of that period confined their remarks within a narrower circle than those of a later date, their information relating more especially to the political and leading elements of the history of the time, seldom polluting their columns with low gossip and irrelevant matter. As is well known, the spirit of political party seldom ran higher than at that period, and during no era of England's history was there ever a more talented body of public statesmen, of different shades of political opinion, than in that of George the Third. The names of such men as Pitt, Fox, Burke, Sheridan (and many more might be added) are sufficient to tell what a storm of eloquence was likely to arise when they came into collision, and there is little doubt but party feeling, in the heat of debate, and from other causes, often led even those highly talented men into dangerous extremes.

Tracing the process of public prints, in number and quality, since that time, and marking the two extremes, the contrast is very great. Instead of one man reading the news of a *weekly paper* to a *collected village*, as at that time, perhaps there is scarce a man in town or country now who has not at least *one daily* paper at his own fireside. This is the other extreme, and has its drawbacks. Newspapers were too scarce then, and are now too plenty - so as to be, to a certain extent, a nuisance. The extent to which the freedom of the press has been sanctioned by law, has been much abused by unscrupulous and selfish men, and has misled numbers of readers who "tak' for gospel what the spaeman gies." Many of those second-sighted leaders, fixing their eye on some glorious Utopia, and desirous to share its blessings with all who put trust in them, start a paper, in which they circulate whatever they think will tend to draw subscribers, no matter for its soundness. And to reach this land of Goshen nothing needs to be provided, but something to be cast away. It is only necessary to shake off all trammels of creeds, tests, and all such old wives' fables, by which our fathers were held in bondage, and all will be well. Another evil arising from the great supply is the tendency it has to occupy too much time, which might be more profitably employed.

Perhaps the publicity given in this way to matters which, strictly speaking, ought to be respected as private property, such as the affairs of State and family matters, is not the least of the evils arising from such babbling gossip. The Queen of England cannot change her bedroom, nor a gypsy rob a henroost, but all Europe knows it next morning. A ship-of-war cannot be designed in the private office of the naval engineer, nor a word spoken by a Privy Councillor, but every court in Christendom knows of it in twenty-four hours. A royal prince cannot *innocently* spend an hour now and then in private with a nobleman's wife, nor a coal-heaver be fined five shillings and costs for being drunk and disorderly, but it becomes public property in a few hours. Now, one part of this information is positively hurtful, and the other of no real importance to the world at large, and could well be dispensed with.

CHAPTER VI.

GOOD roads and suitable vehicles for the transmission of person and property go a great way in civilising and otherwise improving a country. Wigtonshire, like all other parts of Scotland, has made good progress during the present century in this as in other things.

Perhaps one reason why the roads in that county, in former days, had such a decided propensity for passing right over every hill in their progress, might arise from the fact that, with the exception of a few in the parish of Kirkinner, surveyed by the great Basil, Lord Daer, the greater part of all the others were lined off by the gentlemen of the locality through which they passed. And, no doubt, the finding of the soundest bottom with the lightest surface, naturally requiring less labour in forming and least surface metal, was a primary object in adopting these lines. All swamps and marshes were carefully shunned, and a body of solid rock with a smooth surface, cropping up, was a condition of things thankfully made available. On passing through bottoms and level spaces, which they could not always avoid, if a boulder came in their way, unless it stood very much above the common level, it must not be disturbed - it needed no gravel, and would wear well. I lately had a solitary stroll along the old turnpike road to Whithorn, along which kings and nobles have passed centuries ago, to do penance at the shrine of good old St. Ninian at Candida Cassa, but which has been disused for more than half-a-century. It runs from the farm of Carsgown to Bladnoch Bridge, passing over a succession of low rocky heights, the greater portion of it consisting of the natural rocks, very little of it needing any surface metal, and is a fair specimen of the old Galloway highways. As was naturally the case, the difficulty and expense of transport over such roads, in the clumsy carts of the time, with a heavy squeaking at every jolt, like a pig in a gate, was very great, and required at least the power of three horses to do what would now be done with great ease by one.

If the description I have given of the old high way is a correct one - and a few yet alive can affirm it - I need not say one word in favour of to-day, it is quite visible to every one; and the improvement in construction and number of carriages of all descriptions has kept pace with, perhaps even exceeded, the improvements in the roads. At the time to which I can look back, there were only five gentlemen between Bladenoch and Borrowhead who had a carriage superior to a farmer's dung-cart, and the passing of one of them through the village drew every one who could crawl to the street to gaze and wonder. In those times, the highest point of refinement in travelling in the west of Scotland, by the middle classes, was on horseback; and on Sunday and gala days a pad was strapped to the saddle, on which were perched the farmer and his "better half." But let Burns describe it.

> "Here, farmers gash in riding graith,
>   Gaed hoddan by their cottars;
> There, swankies young, in braw braid claith,
>   Are springin' owre the gutters.
> The lasses, skelpin barefit, thrang,
>   In silks and scarlets glitter;
> Wi' sweet-milk cheese in mony a whang,
>   An' farls baked wi' butter -
>   Fu' crump that day."

CHAPTER VII.

AS the changes that have taken place on the face of the county, generally, during the last eighty years - from the steady progress of the most approved system of agriculture - are among the things which I could wish to bring under the notice of the present generation; and, as in no other part of the county has a greater change taken place than in the holm portion of the Baldoon Estate, I shall begin with the low land bordering the Wigton Bay.

How many centuries may have rolled over since that portion of land formed part of the bay of Wigton, no man can tell; but that it did at one time form such a portion, no man can disprove. It extends nearly four miles north and south along the lovely bay. Its breadth at the north end-say, two miles - narrowing to a few hundred yards at Orchardton, on the south. When I first saw it, it was an immense unbroken field of pasture land, the then proprietor - Basil, Lord Daer - being just commencing operations by dividing it into fields of different sizes, by double ditches, with stripes of plantation, which still remain. He also intersected the land with two excellent roads, and built a few excellent cottages, out of one of which our family was driven by the sea, as aforesaid. No doubt centuries had passed since that great field had been thrown up into ridges, varying from fifteen to fifty feet broad, with corresponding spaces, while the angle of elevation was wonderfully well kept up - say, one foot in height for every eight of base. In rainy weather the spaces between the ridges were so flooded that a canoe would have been useful when crossing. They ran from the hard land in an unbroken curved line into the sea at high-water - the tide ebbing out nearly three miles, leaving that extent of sand at low water. Great credit is due to the memory of the men of those days for their persevering exertions in battling with the ocean, by throwing up those huge ridges over such an extent of surface, in order to preserve that rich portion of land left them by the receding of the great sea. How long they remained in peaceable possession previous to 1790 - the period when I first became familiar with it - none can tell; but, at that time, old Neptune had assumed the aggressive, by washing away the ends of the ridges, insidiously stealing his way over his ancient domain. One monster ridge claims particular attention. It occupied a space nearly in the middle of the strath, and was a full mile in length, much broader and higher than the others, and was called *par excellence*, ''Rosie's Rigg.'' Tradition tells us that it acquired this name from the fact that a certain *myth*, called Rosie, cut the whole of an excellent crop on this ridge with a hook in one day. Now, this being a feat that no merely human arm could have performed, the said Rosie must have had something ''no' cannie'' about her. We know, ''if ancestry can be aught believed,'' that different classes of beings of rather a visionary cast were in early times seen in the locality, as in every other quarter of the country.

It is not possible to say whether Rosie was a fairy, a brownie, or a fire or water kelpie, perhaps a cross between some of the parties; but she must have been of some note in the district, as a lovely green bank facing the sea on the farm of Orchardton, at the end of the strath, is called Rosie's Brae, and a delightful spring at its foot also bears her name. Those ridges lay undisturbed till early in the present century, when drains were put in the spaces, and a gradual levelling process by the plough, reducing the whole strath into a flat plain of as rich wheat-bearing land as any in the kingdom.

With a few feeble, though praiseworthy attempts at improvement, agriculture was in a very low state in Wigtonshire at the end of the eighteenth century. Great quantities of surface water lay undisturbed from generation to generation, every little hollow having its loch of water, swarming with leeches and water fowl, and every little burn alive with fine spotted trout. Numerous marshes of all sizes, covered with rushes, other portions with dwarf alder, slae-thorn, and all manner of obnoxious things that delight in moisture abounded through the whole country, imparting to it a dreary and desolate aspect.

This was not all that needed mending; - black cattle and sheep at that time forming the staple commodity of the farmer. There were large patches of whins - already described - allowed to keep possession of portions of the most fertile spots in the county undisturbed by plough or hoe. This was the state of things generally, up to the time when the lands of Baldoon fell, by purchase, into the possession of the house of Galloway, when an event occurred which produced a magical change from the old system. In fact, a new era was introduced. This was brought about by the letting of the Baldoon lands for a term of nineteen years, by public competition in the court-house of Wigton, when rents were offered that never had been dreamed of by a Galloway farmer. Farm rents had, in the course of ages, crept up from a few pounds a year to a few hundreds; but on that occasion farms of moderate extent were let at above two thousand a year. Men of energy and capital came on the field, and a great change passed over the spirit of the people's dreams generally. The old clumsy wooden plough became a thing of the past, iron ones were substituted with machinery "o' a' dimensions, shapes, and metals," for clearing and pulverising the soil; draining and fencing went on with an energy truly surprising. The old rickety thatched hovels were quickly superseded by large commodious slated houses, with offices to correspond; surface water disappeared; brambles, rushes, whins, broom, all and sundry got notice to quit. A general polishing of surface eagerly commenced, which has been regularly going on in all parts of the county, but which now has little more to do.

It would not be doing justice to the home tenant to imagine that all the merit of the great improvement was due to the foreigners, who got farms on that occasion. They certainly did their part, and showed a good example; but, as a proof of the quality of the home element, only three farms then let remain in the hands of the heirs of the contractors in 1806, and they are pure Gallovedians, with not a gill of foreign blood in their veins. The farms alluded to are North and South Balfern, and Eastmains of Baldoon, while not a single outsider kept possession to the end of the lease.

The winding up of a forty years' war, the last act of which was played out on the field of Waterloo, on Sunday, 18th June, 1815 - where the immortal Wellington unharnessed that second Atila, Napoleon, and restored peace to the world - produced its natural effects. However desirable, in a general way, peace might be, from the tendency it had to lower the price of agricultural produce, it proved very trying on the tenants who held land on the old rental; and the disastrous state of matters consequent on the unprecedented cold and rainy nature of the summer and harvest of 1816, which stands without a parallel in the memory of any living man, - perhaps scarcely equalled in history, - proved a heavy blow and great discouragement to the honest farmer; and the wonder was not that a few were ruined, but that so many weathered the storm. The well-known leniency of the noble family of Galloway, and, no doubt, that of other proprietors, came nobly out on that occasion, and saved the credit of many. The season was truly a gloomy one; with little exception, a heavy mass of dark cloud hung over the world like a winding-sheet, through which the sun was very seldom visible, and when a glimpse of it was got through a ragged rift, there was a sickly glare about it, which rendered the visit scarcely a compliment. Out of these clouds too, poured down all but an incessant fall of heavy cold rain.

On early farms the crops partially ripened well in to September and October; but in upland districts thousands of acres never ripened at all, and were never cut, as, when the rain took off, snows and frost set in, which rendered it impossible to gather them.

Having occasion to visit Stoney Kirk on the 22d November of that year, being a clear, frosty day, I well remember when passing through Mochrum and Luce to witness all along numbers of people dragging portions of grain from under the frozen snow; and, I also recollect (it being the first I ever bought) of paying six shillings and threepence for one stone of very indifferent oatmeal, in the spring of 1817, in consequence of the disastrous character of the previous year.

During the first fourteen years of the writer's life, from 1786 till 1800, famine periods - proceeding from various causes-occurred, during which, had it not been for the noble way in which the wealthier portion of the community came forward and advanced money to bring breadstuffs into the country, death from starvation would, in many cases, have been inevitable. It was nobly done, and ought to hallow the memory of the generous givers in the mind of every right-thinking man. The imported stuff, generally, consisted of oatmeal, flour, rice, and maize; and was put into stores; families classed and numbered; a competent quantity allotted to each weekly; and the price reduced to suit their respective circumstances from the money subscribed. During one of these periods, a very severe one, - the winter of 1799 and spring of 1800 - I was in farm service, and remember well that on coming home on the Sundays my kind-hearted mother always had a basin of rice and milk prepared for me as a treat, and to this day the homely dish is a particular favourite. It ought to be a matter of much thankfulness that none of those disastrous visitations have been experienced in this country for a long time back. Different reasons may be given, under Providence, for the fending off of the dire calamity. The highly improved state of agriculture; the very great extent of surface available in excess of the olden time; and the facility of procuring supplies by steam and other powers that have made our brethren in China and other faraway lands almost our door neighbours; "with other appliances and means to boot," may prevent the return of those evil days.

CHAPTER VIII.

IT is quite obvious to every one who has looked at the subject with the least attention, that a very marked change has gradually taken place in the climate of this country during the period under our observation. I am not an astronomer, nor sufficiently acquainted with natural philosophy, to give reasons for this change, but the fact itself "winna ding, and darna be disputed." One thing is well known that, for many years back, the mariner's compass has varied considerably in its polar attraction, which seems as if some hitch had taken place which might partly account for the change of the climate. Were it not that I might subject myself to the sneer of better informed men, I would relate a curious tale, but one, that I have the temerity to say, I quite believe to be a true one.

The tale was told me many years ago by one of the shrewdest and most observant old men I ever had the pleasure of being acquainted with, and who dabbled much in geography. He held a farm in the parish of Wigton in the latter end of the eighteenth century, and retired into the burgh to "adjust his mantle ere he fell."

The first summer he came into Wigton burgh to reside he chanced to be on the highest point of the hill on which the town stands, on the longest day, just as the sun was setting. There is a small hill to the north-west of the hill of Wigton, in the parish of Penningham, about six miles off, called the Fell of Baraar, which juts up, like a hay rick, to a moderate height, but of no great breadth.

On the occasion mentioned, the old gentleman noticed that the sun set in an exact line with the south side of the fell, and the thought struck him that he would take notice on the same day yearly as long as he lived, to see if it would still set at the same point.

He kept his resolution, and, very shortly before his death, he told me that the earth had gradually gone round to the west, just so far that, on his last observation, the sun set in an exact line with the *north* side of the fell, corresponding exactly with the western variation of the compass.

> "I cannot say how the truth may be;
> I tell the tale as 'twas told to me."

From whatever cause, a decided change has taken place in the nature of the winter seasons during my own recollection, especially in the severity of the winter frosts. During the nineties of the bygone century, winters of frost and snow occurred of severity enough to make an Esquimeaux shiver in his bearskin.

One of those Arctic seasons is fresh in my memory. My father was living on a farm in Kirkcolm, in the Rhinns, under the late John Drew, Esq. The winter set in early in November, with a heavy snow storm, immediately followed by severe frost, which continued, with very partial breaks, well into March; and I have heard my father often tell that he finished planting potatoes the following summer on the 22d June. And great numbers of water-fowl from Lochryan were found dead in the frozen-up ditches, where they went in search of food and fresh water: and many of them alighted on the frozen snow, who never could rise again, all of them reduced to bundles of bones and feathers.

Winters of a similar kind, of less or more severity, continued with longer and longer intervals of milder ones up to about 1830 - two of the most intense being the winters and springs of 1825 and 1826 - preceded by summers of intense heat and drought. I was an enthusiastic curler, consequently frosty winters were special favourites, and the occasional lamentation over an unexpected defeat, and the far more pleasing task of rejoicing at, and exulting over, a victory, kept alive in the mind of the keen curler his victories and defeats, as well as the very nature of the days on which the battles were fought. To this I attribute the photographic distinctness in my mind's eye, not only of my victories and defeats, but even the very nature of the air, ice, and sky, on special occasions, throughout many years. From all this I am able to bear out one peculiar aspect, which the northern quarter of the sky assumed during intense frost, and which, to my certain knowledge, has not been seen in Scotland for the last forty years. I allude to a deep blue, or rather black, shade, which arose in the northern horizon as soon as the sun began to decline in the afternoon, while all the rest of the sky maintained a brilliant blue, as pure as that of Italy.

It rose to a height of about twenty degrees in the centre, dying away in rainbow form east and west to the horizon. About the year 1830 a palpable change came over the appearance of the sky in frosty weather - the above blue, a token of good ice next day, no longer remained to cheer the curler's heart, by assuring him, as he strode home, exulting over a victory, and anticipating another next day over a rival parish, that the ice would be all he could desire. No such pleasant "token of a goodly day to-morrow" remains for the poor curler. It has "gone, and left not a rack behind." Instead of this cheering token, a thin yellow sickly looking haze hangs about, even during the hardest frost we have had since the time I have stated; and, what is remarkable, the change took place simultaneously with the *potato disease* - whether or not that sickly-looking atmosphere had any hand in destroying the potato I do not pretend to say.

CHAPTER IX

BEFORE proceeding farther in marking the changes in the rural districts, it would be unpardonable to pass over that most remarkable hill, on whose eastern shoulder good taste has hung the ancient Borough of Wigton, from which all the Macher or eastern portion of the county can be seen at one glance.

This lovely hill stands on the west side of the north end of the Wigton Bay. Its base occupies about a square mile, with an elevation of between two and three hundred feet above the sea level. It is covered with a deep, rich soil, as green as an emerald, rising abruptly on the east and west sides, more moderately on the other two, is accessible by five good roads, and the view from it is magnificent. With the exception of one point, the hill is flattened on the top, as if the top had been shaven off, with a slight inclination to the south and east on which the town stands.

On the west shoulder a point of rock crops up with a thin stratum of green surface, on the apex of which the good people of Wigton have done themselves much credit by erecting a handsome monument in memory of the two heroic women who were drowned at the foot of the hill for adherence to the dictates of their own conscience in matters of religion, by cruel and intolerant men. From the site of this monument one of the finest and most extensive views in the county, or perhaps from any point of the same elevation anywhere, can be obtained. Looking to the east of the bay, a chain of heathery mountains of considerable height is seen, rising abruptly at Kirkdale Point in Kirkcudbrightshire, about eight miles distant, as the crow flies. From this point the chain, with slight breaks, runs away due north for a distance of fifty miles, melting away far into Ayrshire.

Turning south-eastward, at a distance of fifty miles, the huge Skiddaw and Shapfell in Cumberland send their brown heads far away up into the higher regions, the view extending into Lancashire. Due south the whole of the eastern portion of the county is under the eye, in addition to a portion of St. George's channel, in which seems to float the Isle of Man. This lovely isle - if we may put any faith in Irish tradition - took flight out of the space now occupied by Loch Neagh in the Emerald isle, and settled where it now stands; let us hope, regenerated by the dip. Turning westward, the channel is seen away to the coast of Ireland, with the blue mountains of Morn in the distance; northwards, the brown heathery uplands, for thirty miles, to the "Braes of Balloch," split as if to allow the road to Ayr a free passage, every turn of the eye - like the shade of a kaleidoscope bringing up some new and interesting change of scenery. One feature in the landscape must not be overlooked - the profusion of little green hills similar to that on which the spectator is standing strewn so liberally, like unripe oranges - above one hundred of which may be seen from Wigtonhill; and the individual who would not be charmed by the view does not deserve to have eyes at all.

For several years up into the present century, the water of Bladenoch, as soon as it entered into the bay, turned due north, sweeping close along the foot of the hill, forming a harbour for the district, at Croftanree, for vessels of moderate draught of water. Flowing away with a graceful sweep to join the Cree about half-way down the bay. In this graceful bend of the Bladenoch was perpetrated by cruel and unmerciful men one of the most cold-blooded and murderous acts that stand recorded in the history of nations. Yes, from this spot took their flight the redeemed spirits of Margaret M'Laughlan and Margaret Wilson, two of the noblest spirits ever carried to Heaven in a chariot of fire. A certain Sheriff Napier (of whom better things might have been expected) has stepped much out of his way to ignore the whole affair; but never did a base libel on a thing of truth meet with a more calm and triumphant refutation than what has been administered to him in that admirable pamphlet by the Rev. Archibald Stewart of Glasserton. A kindred spirit is shown by that highly talented man, Robert Chambers, in his "Picture of Scotland;" and it is to be regretted that through the whole of that clever book, where ever the subject of martyrdom comes in his way he treats it with much levity; with more wit and prejudice than truth and charity. He says they were *girls* - one of them was certainly a girl of eighteen, and a noble girl too; but Margaret M'Laughlan was rather an *old girl* in her seventy-eighth year; and he expresses a doubt "whether a woman of any age has a right to think for herself on religious and political subjects." This is a supposition so monstrous as to require no refutation; and I will leave it to the world to judge him as he has judged the martyrs. It is an incontrovertible fact, that, though the *persecuted* might not always be in the right, the *persecutor* was *always* in the *wrong*.

In no part of the county is there a spot on which a greater change has taken place than in the bend of the Bladenoch at Croftanree, where those stakes were fixed to which the innocent victims were chained to await the coming tide. Where vessels used to load and discharge, cattle are now grazing, and a splendid body of land reclaimed from the mighty deep. But the marvellous transformation of the town must not be forgot. When I became first acquainted with it - in the last ten years of the last century - the greatest number of the houses were of a very homely character, thatched and one-storey high, each house having a *midden* in front on the ample street. The main street was a parallelogram, say, in a roughway, of ninety yards wide, by two hundred in length. A space in the centre, two thirds of the length and thirty yards broad, was paved with large land stones like an old Roman road; while a small stream of water, which arose on the north side of the town, ran unmolested across the upper end. Across the lower or east end, stood the court and market house - a very respectable one for its time - with a tower and spire; and at the upper end of the causeway stood a tall freestone cross. But perhaps the *middens* were the most peculiar feature of the place; there they lay in a row on each side, in all their ''composition of villanous smells,'' undisturbed: good old Provost Burton's, one of the richest and most unsavoury of the lot. I beg leave to give Robert Chambers's version of the *midden* case from his, ''Picture of Scotland.'' Chambers, when speaking of the New Square and Bowling Green which now occupy the centre of the old street of Wigton, says - ''This is altogether a wonderfully fine thing and quite unexampled in Scotland. Its merit must be doubly appreciated by the stranger, when he is informed that the space which it occupies was the site of the great common dunghill of the people of Wigton. An amusing thing is told in regard to the former use and purpose of the place. Upon the occasion of an election, when it was found impossible to clear the ground of its vast stercoraceous encumbrance in proper time, boards were laid over it, and upon these were erected tables, at which a great body of honest burghers and wily politicians sat down to a public dinner. Perhaps so many honourable men were never before known to dine upon a dunghill.'' I will not attempt to enumerate the many changes in a right direction that have taken place since I first saw it; but any one who reads my first impressions of it, and compares the state of matters then and now, must see and rejoice at the wonderful improvement.

CHAPTER X.

DURING all bygone time, including my early days, the belief was cherished in the existence of various kinds of beings of a middle class, friendly or hostile to man according to the class - fairy, brownie, fire or water kelpie, &c.- as the case might be; and their existence, haunts, habits, and instances of good or evil tricks was the engrossing topic of conversation whenever a gossiping party met in the winter evenings in Galloway, as in all other parts of Scotland; and the district, was rich in such lore. The brownie tribe seems not to have been a prolific one, not by any means so numerous as the fairy; but they, certainly, were, the most friendly and useful of the lot. They were so - not only as being less mischievous, but as actually very friendly, and, in many instances, very useful.

Witness the "Brownie of Bladenoch," a poem that has immortalised the memory of my old friend William Nicholson, "the packman," who, for many years, made the glens of Galloway vocal with the sound of his bagpipe, and enlivened many a hearth with his "legendary lore" and personal eccentricities. He published a volume of poetry, which is well known in the whole of the south and west of Scotland; but the "Brownie," as was said by the late talented editor of the *Dumfries Courier*, Mr M'Dairmid, who reviewed the book, constituted him a poet. The fairy family seem, on the contrary, to be of a more selfish and homeward-bound character - in fact, very annoying and mischievous. Of this numberless instances are given us of a mother having been whipt off in the night, leaving her good man fast asleep, with the infant at his back, quite unconscious of the abominable abstraction, while the poor woman is detained for months suckling a young fairy in some dune or stronghold of a rascally old fairy; and only returned when his, hopeful offspring can be spoon fed. And worse still - they have been known to whip away a blooming baby out of its cradle, and substitute a changeling elf to torment and fret the life out of the poor mother.

The kelpies, and similar tribes of the *fay* family, were wholly given to mischief.

For many years bypast, when entering into conversation with a genuine believer in the existence and character of the whole visionary families - the belief in which has been gradually losing ground - did you ask him the simple question, "If ever they had an existence, why not exist now?" he would gravely give you as a sufficiently good reason, that it is in consequence of the more extensive diffusion of the gospel, which they hate as bitterly as their master hates holy water. Now, in order to test the soundness and consistency of his theory, just seem satisfied with his answer, and introduce the state of the religious and moral character of the late and present times, and he will as gravely assure you that things are getting worse every day - every generation worse than the one before consequently no time so utterly graceless as the present. Now, some people fail to see the force and consistency of the two averments. There is perhaps a natural tendency in the young mind to believe in the supernatural, and when that disposition is strengthened by early gossiping of marvellous stories, it must be next to impossible to disabuse the mind, either by ridicule or philosophy. When it is well known that such men as Dr. Johnson, Dr. Chalmers, and thousands of others of equally high talent, whom we meet with in history, were quite unable to " pluck the old woman from their heart," how can it be expected that common sinners are able to do so? Thousands there are who sneer at and hold up to ridicule others whom they know to believe in such things, who themselves would much rather go supperless to bed in their own room than pass the night, in any circumstances, in a chamber of a doubtful character; and, when travelling late, would rather prefer a road, although a mile or two longer, to one by the side of which a "drucken Charlie" had "brak's neck-bane," or a "Mungo's mither" had "hang'd hersel'." In proof that such a weakness exists, even in the minds of, in other respects, sound-minded, right-thinking men, who have not the shadow of a belief in the return of departed spirits in any shape, they will in certain positions find a sense of dread strike them which they neither can account for nor easily shake off. This must proceed from a natural bias towards what is called superstitions, strengthened by listening to the ghostly gossipings of early life.

I do not pretend to say that I am one of those strong-minded individuals, but I will say that I as firmly believe in the non-appearance of departed spirits as I do that they once were united to bodies and conversed with me here on earth, and that beings of a middle class never had an existence at all. And yet I as candidly confess that in certain cases during a long life I have been under the influence of a panic which I could neither shake off nor account for, although my belief at the time was unshaken as to the absurdity of the alarm. One instance I have previously given in my "Sailor Life" - the affair of the rolling calf in Kingston, Jamaica - and I shall so far show the influence of the feeling which once more came over me in later times, in proof of my perfect conviction that there was no real cause for it. Having occasion to attend a cousin's wedding in Barrochan, in Mochrum, in the autumn of 1812, on the breaking up of the party, at one o'clock on a bright, starlight morning, late in September, I started on a walk of five miles on my way home to my father's house at Milldriggan. Three miles of the way was of a very rough, moory character - "through mosses, waters, slaps, and stiles," and execrable roads, if roads they might be called. I reached the public highway leading from Wigton to Port William, within two miles from home, the most pleasant part of the journey, and having walked very fast, was in a profuse state of perspiration. Up to this time I had as little dread of anything human or diabolical as if I had been all the while at sermon in the parish church. I had just passed the last house before coming to the two small clumps of plantation at the entrance of the avenue to Barnbarrow House, when, in an instant, a sensation of terror struck me, to an extent I never either before or since experienced. I was perspiring copiously, when in one moment I felt a chill all over me, as if a bucket of ice water had been emptied on my head, and a feeling as if my hat was rising from my head, and I actually put my hand up to keep it from, as I imagined, falling off. All this was going on while I had neither heard a sound nor seen an object that was not common and familiar, nor had I firmness to ..

> "Glower roun' wi' prudent care,
> Lest bogles caught me unaware."

On the contrary, I stared right ahead to keep my line of vision as circumscribed as possible. In this state I continued mechanically to walk rapidly on, shivering, as if in an ague, till I passed the bridge of Barglass - the whole enchanted distance gone over being about one-fourth of a mile - when the childish sensation went off as quickly as it came on, leaving me much ashamed of the whole affair.

I reached home all right, changed my clothes, and walked back over the same ground on my way to the farm of Boreland, where I was a harvester, where I arrived just about daylight; nor did the slightest weakness ever annoy me for a moment. The feeling might have crossed my mind of a white lady having been frequently seen in the neighbourhood of Barnbarrow, though I do not remember of it being the case when the dark hour came on. Even had that been the case I might also have remembered that she was *laid*, or conjured, long before my weak fit for "a hunner year and mair."

Granting myself to have been an ass in this instance, and a few others, I find much consolation in thinking I had gone astray in very respectable company, as I find many of the cleverest men of bygone times have been occasionally annoyed by twinges from the same complaint, and indirectly acknowledged its power. The lighter and more visionary portion of the machinery with which superstition manages to carry on its work may safely be raised as food for merriment, although true believers in fairy lore are exceedingly cautious in speaking disrespectfully of them, particularly in the vicinity of their supposed haunts. Allowing this, yet it must not be forgot that an immense difference exists between the real nature and occasional visits of "a fay" from fairyland, and those of a disembodied human soul - allowing such things to be possible in any case - the one being less than nothing and altogether vanity, while the other is a stern reality and has an eternal duration. It is impossible, when speaking on this subject, to pass over that unequalled burst of language and feeling put into the mouth of Hamlet by Shakespeare in the conjuration to his father's ghost:-

"Angels and ministers of grace defend us!
Be thou a spirit of health or goblin damn'd.
Bring with thee airs from heaven, or blasts from hell,
Be thy intents wicked or charitable,
Thou com'st in such a questionable shape,
That I will speak to thee: I'll Call thee Hamlet,
King, Father, Royal Dane. O, answer me!
Let me not burst in ignorance! but tell,
Why thy canonized bones, hearsed in death,

Have burst their cerements! why the sepulchre,
Wherein we saw thee quietly inurn'd,
Hath op'd his ponderous and marble jaws,
To cast thee up again! What may this mean,
That thou, dead corse! again in complete steel,
Revisit'st thus the glimpses of the moon,
Making light hideous; and we fools of nature,
So horribly to shake our disposition
With thoughts beyond the reaches of our souls?
Say what is this? Wherefore? What should we do?''

And it would be equally unpardonable to overlook the poetic power and beauty of the dialogue in Home's Tragedy of Douglas, in the centre of a grove at midnight, ending with -

''In such a place as this,
At such an hour,
If ancestry can be in ought believ'd,
Descending spirits have convers'd with men,
And told the secrets of the world unknown.''

It is quite true that a great weakening in the faith of the million in the existence and power of the ''fay'' tribe has taken place during the present century; the snake is not quite dead, however, it is only scotch'd. The belief in all its entirety was a very harmless delusion, and a very amusing and pleasant element in the gossip of the winter evenings in the happy homes of the Scottish peasantry. The belief in such things was merely shadows of fancy, teazing or amusing as the case might be, without affecting the conscience at all. Far different, however, from the shadows that haunted the guilty mind of the crook-back'd tyrant in dreams in his tent on the field of Shrewsbury, when he declared -

"Shadows to-night
Have struck more terror to the soul of Richard.

> Than can the substance of ten thousand men.''

So true it is -

> "Suspicion haunts the guilty mind,
> The thief thinks every bush an officer."

I, for one, believe that superstition is as universally diffused, in one shape or another, through the whole human race, as air throughout our atmosphere.

I have seen the effects of its power over the mind of the naked African savage, and I have read of its effects on the minds of some of the highest learned and talented men the world can boast of; and though many are ashamed of it, and *deny* it, they, to a man, *feel* it, and are, less or more, affected by its influence. There is a higher and more respectable kind of superstition, however, which deserves a more serious and more reverent mode of treatment, although I believe that much even of that class is equally as visionary and unsubstantial as the other:- I mean the return of departed spirits to this earth, as no positive proof, setting miracles aside, has ever been brought out, to establish the fact; nor would it serve any good purpose; for, "if we believe not Moses and the Prophets, neither would we persuaded though one rose from the dead." Respecting the state of a departed spirit, the most natural supposition seems to be, that the moment of its separation from the body, terminates its business in this world; that it immediately passes to a place suitable for its disembodied state; abiding the hour when a suitable body will be prepared for it - until which time, a great gulf is fixed, over which it cannot pass, but must remain as entirely unacquainted with things of earth, as we are with things in their abode abiding the hour when all secrets will be revealed. Nor is it likely that those who are in a state of happiness would desire to return nor, that those, in an opposite state would be allowed to do so.

CHAPTER XI.

THE excessive expenditure consequent on the extraordinary war brought on by the Revolution in France in 1792, and the previous struggle with America, obliging the British Government to tax the country to an extent never before dreamt of, gave rise to a spirit of discontent and opposition of a dangerous character. As has been already noticed, every article on which a tax was laid went up to enormous prices, and a contraband trade commenced with France, Holland, and the Channel Islands of Guernsey, Jersy, and other places, to an extent never before known in the South of Scotland. A royalty was at that time held by charter over the Isle of Man by the Duke of Athole, since purchased by the Government for £20,000, exempting the Island from certain duties on the importation of certain foreign commodities to which all other parts of the country were subjected. That charter also rendered the Isle a city of refuge to debtors from other places, who could reside there in defiance of all whom it might concern; but they could not leave it without a pass from the Governor; and numbers took the benefit of the charter. As might naturally be expected, the Island became a safe depot for any quantity of contraband stuff but they could not *export* without paying duty.

Independent of this city of refuge, there was also established on the east shore of the Bay of Luce, opposite the Isle, by a lot of farmers and others at Clone, on the estate of Sir William Maxwell, of Monreith, a very extensive smuggling business, importing large quantities of stuff. as above mentioned. The goods naturally consisted of that description on which the tax pressed most heavily, and gave the best chance of profit to the adventurer.

They principally consisted of brandy, wine, gin, rum, tea, silks, lace, gloves, playing cards, &c., of which a constant supply was kept up by fast sailing crafts, under the general name of Buccars, - the many hair-breadth escapes of which from the Prince Edward revenue cutter (Captain Cook), stationed at Isle of Whithorn, formed the. engrossing topic of conversation all over the county.

The principal agent in the shipping department was the celebrated old Dutch skipper, Captain Yeakins, whose name is since immortalised by Sir Walter Scott, in his charming tale of "Guy Mannering,"' as Dick Heatrick.

Yeakins commanded a large lugger-rigged craft, called "The Flora" celebrated for her fast-sailing quality, an indispensable virtue in her line of business. From among many such *tales* I beg leave to give one of the "touch-and-go" escapes of the Flora from the fangs of Captain Cook; and, let me say, that the tale was told me by one who was a seaman on board the Prince Edward, and who by no means relished the fact of the Flora getting so cleverly off.

The Flora had just discharged the bulk of her cargo at the Clone - perhaps intending to call on the Kirkmaiden shore with the rest, and stood away down the Bay, towards the Borrowhead, on purpose to catch the first of the strong ebb tide which hurries through between Borrowhead and Isle of Man, from the coast of Cumberland, Solway Firth, and Wigton Bay, into the Irish Channel, to carry him out of Luce Bay.

The wind was light, and right in his teeth, or he would have stood away at once for the Big Scars to get round the Mull of Galloway before daylight, and not have ventured in such close quarters with his well-known enemy, the Prince Edward, who, he knew, was lying in the Isle of Whithorn harbour, close to the Borrowhead.

About sunrise, which is often the case in calm weather, the wind died away, and left the good ship Flora a helpless log, almost in the very jaws of her enemy. The out-look from Tondergie sighted the old craft as soon as daylight came, and soon, to the consternation of the smugglers, the cutter made her appearance, sweeping out of the harbour. It was dead calm - the tide acting equally on both the vessels, carrying them to the south-westward.

There was nothing for it but the Flora to out sweeps (long oars), and make the best of her way, everything depending on who would catch the breeze first when it arose. If it came at once fresh from the east, Yeakins was a ruined man.

As they were about two miles apart, the short carronades of the cutter could not harm him, so that if the Flora could keep her distance with the sweeps till the breeze came, she was safe. Captain Cook seeing no chance of taking the cutter alongside of the Flora, despatched two well-armed boats to try and take her by boarding, and it was not long till they were within hail of the smuggler.

The Flora was well manned and well armed, and the old skipper loaded two of his carronades with grape shot, and pointing them at the boats, hailed, warning them that if they came nearer he would fire into them. The officer in charge of the boats answered by ordering him to "haul down his colours and submit to His Majesty's cutter, Prince Edward."

Yeakins immediately answered - "Sheer off, or I'll sink you - bring the cutter alongside and I will tell you what I will do. I cannot be responsible to my employers in delivering up the Flora to a boat's crew."

The officer considering "discretion to be the best part of valour," returned to the cutter - about which time a slight breeze came down in cat's paws from the south-east, off the Cumberland Hills.

The Prince Edward caught the breeze a few minutes before the smuggler, and began to creep up, and commenced blazing away with her bow guns, which only retarded her headway, and did no harm to the lugger. In due time the breeze, which continued freshening, reached the Flora, who began to walk through the water in gallant style. The old veteran skipper having taken the helm himself, ordered all hands to lie down on deck, leaving the cutter hand over-hand; having, as the story goes, thrown his hat and wig overboard as all that Captain Cook was likely to get of the Flora.

In spite of the feeble efforts of a few excisemen to check its progress, and in consequence of the trade being winked at by many of the upper class, and encouraged by others - without which it never could have prospered so well in the country, it flourished for years, till the leading men (Morrison, Gault, and others), became rich. Meantime, the attention of the Government was so much engrossed by the fearful struggle for the very existence of Great Britain as a nation, no time could be spared to *harry* a smuggler's nest.

The suppressing of this trade was "a consummation devoutly to be wished," as it had a very demoralising influence over the whole country, particularly in the neighbourhood of the headquarters of the enemy. Of this district it might almost be said of the inhabitants what Boniface, the publican, affirmed of himself, "that he had lived in Shrewsbury for twenty-eight years, and had not eaten twenty-eight ounces of meat. He ate his ale, he drank his ale, and he always slept on ale." So did the Clone smugglers. They ate their brandy, they drank their brandy, and always slept on it. Open house was kept - the spirits on every farmer's dresser as plenty as buttermilk.

The working principle of the trade was admirably arranged. Spies were stationed in all directions when a Buccar was expected, one on every height along the Mochrum and Glasserton shore; and signals night and day - known by both parties - were shown to warn the coming vessel whether or not it was safe to land. The Exciseman was also on the alert with his glass on the same heights looking out for the expected craft but while he imagined himself *incog.*, more than one eye was upon him in all his motions. And if the Buccar did heave in sight and he made a motion to procure assistance, he was pounced upon by masked men, blind-folded, and placed in comfortable quarters his bread being provided and his brandy sure. The coast being clear, the next morning he was removed in a blind-folded state to some distance and set at liberty. It was also said that if, by accident, he should put his hand into a certain pocket he generally found - to his great surprise no doubt - a handful of "yellow Geordies," which had mysteriously found their way there. Meanwhile, perhaps, one hundred horses each with a couple of ankers - small casks - of brandy or a portion of other goods across his haunches, on which was perched a whiskered ruffian with a pair of pistols in his belt and cutlass by his side, had been despatched to Edinburgh or elsewhere, over moor and moss, as the crow flies. The remainder of the cargo all safely stowed away in cellars known only to the initiated; as the whole district was like a rabbit warren under ground, capable of holding an immense quantity of goods.

Every transgression of a law that works well for the general good of society is wrong, and, according to the law of retributive justice, must come to grief. In conformity with this rule, fell the Clone smuggling. A few of the great drops heralding the coming storm may be given.

In course of time, Morrison got a first-class cutter built and despatched to the Channel Islands under the charge of a son or nephew as supercargo. In the homeward voyage, to escape the king's cutter who, he knew, was cruising in the south Irish Channel to intercept him, young Morrison ran round the south and west of Ireland entering the Irish sea between Giant's Causeway and Scotland. The night was pitch dark, and the young supercargo elated by his success so far, and in high hope of a successful termination of his voyage could brook no advice. They had a strong north west breeze - just what suited them, and the cutter was walking through the water in gallant style, when it was suggested by some one that they must be close on the Whillans of Larne - two large invisible rocks that lie off the coast of Antrim. Morrison, who was in high spirits and anxious to profit by the fair wind, unhappily disregarded the warning, declaring he would carry on, as he was determined to be in a place not necessary to name or the Clone before morning. Melancholy to tell, in a few minutes, the cutter struck the rock and was knocked into splinters. All on board except a man of the name of Thomson were drowned. He having got hold of a piece of wreck, was picked up next morning. Report valued the cutter and cargo at fifteen thousand pounds - the first blow and a heavy one to the Clone smugglers.

An old proverb tells us - "Misfortunes never come singly;" it was verified in the case of the illicit traffic in question, as another soon followed. It had its rise in a struggle that took place for the representation of the Wigtonshire Boroughs in the House of Commons, between Sir William Maxwell of Monreith and Commodore Stewart of Glasserton. In those dark and tyrannical days, as an advanced Liberal would tell us, the contest lasted a whole week, though the franchise was, where it ought to have remained, - in the hands of a small number. At that time it seems to have been the practice for the candidates to parade the streets at certain times, attended with large bodies of their adherents by way of display and bravado. Sir William's followers being chiefly of his Clone tenants; when on meeting the Commodore on the street of Whithorn, the old sailor, who could not let slip the chance of having a hit at the Baronet, exclaimed - ''You are very active to-day, Sir William, with your smugglers at your back." "Yes," replied the Baronet, "if you had been as active when you allowed the Dutch Fleet to pass you off the Dogar Bank, it would have been telling the crown of Britain many a thousand pounds." "I'll suppress the smuggling," was the retort of the Admiral. He laid the case before the Government, and a barracks was built at Port William, a party of soldiers quartered there, and the trade and those who conducted it were ruined - "Troy is no more; and Ilion was a town." It is only very recently that the demoralising effects of the trade have disappeared from the locality in which the headquarters were placed; and which had also, to a greater or less degree, extended over the whole country. As I have before observed, had not the trade been winked at by a majority of those in power, and patronised by the vast numbers of all classes who profited by it, it never could have been prosecuted to such an extent. There, no doubt, were honourable exceptions; but it was notorious that many of them were persons of whom better things might have been expected.

CHAPTER XII.

BY allowing me to borrow a few old world recollections from one who lived in the time, and shared in the privations, and witnessed and bore a part in the scenes he describes, it will serve to introduce the reader into the period when I take up the tale of the agricultural condition of Wigtonshire.

Assuming this indulgence, I can go back one hundred and eighty years into the traditionary lore of my native county - occupying only two lives. A few are yet alive who knew that wonderful old man, Alexander M'Creadie, who, I believe, resided through his long life in the parish of Kirkinner and neighbourhood, and who died in a small cabin on the march of Kirkinner and Sorbie, at the patriarchal age of one hundred and nine years. I knew him well from my infancy as one of the mildest, most honest and unassuming old men that can be imagined. He was a labouring man, a widower, with one son, in my earlier days; which son - then an old man - was gardener to Mr M'Connel, Sheriff at Wigton, and as different from his father as any two things of the same species could possibly be. The son was a shrewd observer of passing events, bitterly sarcastic respecting the characters and opinions of those who differed from him, a decided sceptic in religious matters, a sturdy free-thinker, and one who "moistened his clay" regularly, particularly on Sunday. Being born within a mile of the old man's residence, I knew him well for the first twenty years of my life, and conversed frequently with him on the state of the times, in the days of his youth. His invariable answer to any one who inquired after his health was, "Stirrin, I thank you," or, "I thank you, stirrin." And many times a few young ones of us on calling at the good old man's cabin, or passing him outside, would follow one an other at short distances and ask gravely how he was; we all got the invariable response. Let me say, however, that this was not done in derision, nor in mockery of the venerated old man, as young and old highly respected him, - but by way of a harmless joke. He was of a slight frame of body, and walked with a slight stoop, and seemed like one who had enjoyed excellent health; no such thing as a cough was heard, or difficulty of breathing exhibited; his sight and hearing a little dull, but not to a great extent. He chewed tobacco, and he was frequently to be seen passing into Wigton to procure a supply, a distance of nearly five miles, and returning on the same day, without any particular symptoms of fatigue, and this any time between the hundredth and hundred and seventh year of his age. And I have conversed frequently with him in those years, while he was employed building small drystone walls on the public road-side leading from Wigton to Whithorn. Neither did his mental faculties or memory seem to have suffered much from his extreme old age; his mental powers never had been of a high class, and his education was very limited, but it was pleasant to listen to him telling, in his own simple style, tales of years long gone by, of the manners and customs of his own times. One strange feature in his early reminiscences was the deplorably low state of agriculture and want of roads in the county, and the consequent scarcity and rude quality of the common necessaries of life, particularly among the working classes. Milk and vegetables of a very coarse quality seem to have been the principal resource. Old Saunders told me that he, when a boy, with the other children would gather various kinds of vegetables - potatoes, there were none - and these were boiled up with a small portion of oat or barley meal, food which must have been of a very unpalatable and unsubstantial kind. He spoke also of a plan, often reported to in the summer season, of frequently bleeding the cattle and mixing the blood with meal, forming a kind of bread or *scone*; - and, allow me to say, that I have tasted scones of this kind made by an old woman about 90, as a curiosity, when I was a servant boy in a farm house. She got the blood when the *mert* was killed at Martinmas, but I did not like it. The old man also told me, that his mother had a large "crock" for holding butter-milk, which received a weekly supply, and when he and others of the children would come in asking for something to eat, his mother took the "spurtle" an' rummaged up the milk, and gied us a mouthfu' or twa o' the frod, and we were nae lang oot till we were back again, for by the time we had gaen twa or three loups, we gied a brough or twa, and were as ready as ever for the "crock."

The farm operations also were of a very primitive description. A few acres, at most, in the immediate vicinity of the house was all that, in a general way, was ever thought of as cropping land, being as much as the manure produced by the cattle in winter would top dress, the manure being borne in creels on the backs of the bipeds of the household, as there was not a wheeled machine in the place, or a road to run it on. This favoured spot was called the *fey* and those *fey* spots are still visible on many farms by the richness and black colour of the mould, and the deep green quality of the grass in the early spring.

Respecting the county at that early period, one thing is evident, that a road of a very rude kind, no doubt, existed, whereby hundreds of devotees, from kings to common sinners passed to and from the borders of Ayrshire - vestiges of which are still traceable at intervals, to this day, as I have already noticed in a former article. But with regard to the state of matters in the county in the times I have been speaking of, we will let old Saunders tell his own experience. And, very recently, I was told an anecdote to the very point, by my most esteemed friend, if he will allow me to call him so, the Rev. James Reid, who has faithfully discharged his ministerial duties in the parish of Kirkinner for the last fifty-five years, with whom the old man was a great favourite, That gentleman told me that one time, when talking with Saunders on the state of things in his youth, he told him that on one occasion a number of people were raised, of whom he was one, with implements to pioneer a way across the country to Sir William Maxwell of Monreith's place, for the passage of the first wheel carriage he ever saw in the county, or, I suppose, anywhere else. What a contrast with the present time. And in a conversation with myself, he said that in his youth there was neither "a wee spinnin' wheel" since then used for spinning flax, nor a man's hat, between the braes of Glenapp and the Borrow head - the extreme points of the county south and north. He himself never wore a hat; to the end of his life he wore a broad blue bonnet. On the death of the good old man, the noble Earl of Galloway, at his own expense, and very much to his credit, buried him in the graveyard of his native parish, and erected a handsome monument at the grave, with a characteristic effigy, in stone, of the deceased, with his conspicuous broad bonnet.

The progress of machinery has rendered the "wee wheel" a short-lived article, as I am of opinion it would be difficult to find one at work now within the county. Peace to his memory! If every Gallovedian had the same unostentatious piety, and honest simplicity in moral and political matters, as had my respected old friend, Alexander M'Credie, such vermin as sceptics, rebels, and immoral characters generally would be as scarce in the county now, as men's "hats" and "wee wheels" were in his early days.

CHAPTER XIII.

"Scotland! the land of all I love,
And the land of all that love me;
Land whose green sod my youth has trod,
Whose sod shall lie above me."

THE hardy Caledonian has long been subjected to the insulting sneers of his Southern neighbours, on the rugged and sterile character of his native home, and the love he bears to it. Let them enjoy their harmless merriment "The sports of children satisfy the child." Notwithstanding all their silly mirth, much good has come out of that very barrenness, not only to the hardy natives themselves, but to the world at large. "Necessity is the mother of invention." What was to be done by the natives of such a sterile region but to go earnestly to work and cultivate and improve it - its very sterility acting as a stimulant to perseverance, in order to wring from the reluctant soil what nature had withheld - every fresh exertion improving the physical power of the man, and increasing his knowledge in the art; till in due time he and the art became a model for others.

Besides, nature has so constituted the man that he is as parsimonious in his food and habits as he is indefatigable in his industry. To such an extent is this the case, that, set the stoutest labourer in England alongside of the hardy Scot, let them perform the same amount of work, and live on Scottish fare, and the sneering Saxon will be dead in a month. Take away from him the huge messes of beef, bacon, beans, bread, and allowance of stout; let him breakfast with honest Saunders on a small cogue of brose, and dine with him on *muslin kale*, and for the short time he has to live, he will never laugh any more. The idea may, perhaps, be extravagant; but the sterility of Scotland although to be regretted in so far, 'tis true that in spite of their energy, poor old Caledon cannot shelter all her hardy sons - many of whom are compelled to wander over the world - this very necessity proving beneficial to other lands as they diffuse their skill and energy wherever they go. Scotland is placed as it were for a barrier to protect the north of Europe by an unflinching wall of rocky precipices, against which the great Atlantic breaks with foaming fury; her rugged framework composed of Ben Nevis, Ben Cruachan, Ben Lomond, and many others, towering in awful sublimity and grandeur, like props for the blue canopy overhead, with lochs of surpassing beauty gleaming at their feet, like mirrors to reproduce by reflection the figures of their rugged and gigantic outlines. Byron has brought this out very finely in his contrast of Scottish and English scenery -

> "England, thy beauties are tame and domestic
> To one who has roamed on thy mountains afar;
> Oh, for the scenes that are wild and majestic!
> The steep frowning glories of dark Lochnagar."

And Goldsmith's lovely lines on Switzerland apply equally well to our Highlander respecting his native scenery and love of home -

> "Thus every good his native wilds impart,
> Imprint the patriot passion on his heart;
> And e'en those ills that round his mansion rise
> Enhance the bliss his scanty fund supplies.
> Dear is that shed to which his soul conforms.
> And dear that hill which lifts him to the storms;
> And as a child whom scaring sounds molest,
> Clings close and closer to the nurse's breast -

So the loud torrent, and the whirlwind's roar,
But bind him to his native mountains more.''

So much for Scotland and her hardy sons, who have

"Hearts resolved and hands prepared,
The blessings they enjoy to guard.''

ODDS AND ENDS, CHIEFLY IN RHYME.

Address to the Stormy Petrel.

THE stormy petrel is a small aquatic bird, much resembling our largest swallow both in appearance and in the activity of its motions. It skims along the surface of the ocean like the swallow on a pool; the petrel, however, is web-footed, and can rest on the water. These birds are of a strange wandering character - roaming over the whole of the tropical portion of the Atlantic and Pacific oceans. There is little doubt that they find an abundant supply of food from fish spawn; and I observed that the ship's wake - that is the space of water she passes through- was a favourite place of resort, as they kept sweeping constantly along it, finding, no doubt, that the agitation of the water turned up their food. The wonder is how they live without fresh water, so essential to all other fowls.

They are to be seen plodding on their weary flight a thousand miles from any land as commonly as at other distances.

> Tell me, thou lovely little bird!
> What land thou call'st thine own? -
> Whether Columbo's late found world,
> Or Afric's fiery zone -
> For here thou art half-way between,
> Careering wild and free.
> Hast thou a star to guide thy path
> Across the mighty sea?

Ah, no, sweet bird! it is not so;
    No science guides thy way;
'Tis instinct from a Master power
    Keeps thee from going astray.
In nature's lovely golden chain,
    What link dost thou supply?
For nothing 'ere was made in vain
    To walk, or swim, or fly.

In spawn of fishes floating round
    No doubt thou find'st thy food;
But, when athirst, what quencheth it!
    And what about thy brood?
The gray old salt will gravely tell
    A very wondrous thing,
That incubition thou perform'st
    Beneath thy flying wing,

And how old mother Carey was
    The matron of thy race,
With other tales that quite defy
    All gravity of face.
A thousand miles from any land
    We've met, where sea and sky,
Our little bark, and thou, sweet bird!.
    Were all that met the eye.

The flying fish might rise, indeed,
    In shoals to shun their foe,
Who, bursting up, rose high in air,
    Then plunged down below.
But thou, thou wondrous tiny waif!
    At morning, noon, and night,
Careering onward, onward still,
    In thy untiring flight,

Kept by us aye, as if dispos'd
    The sailor's heart to cheer -
The only living object nigh -
    For which he loves thee dear.

Farewell! a long farewell to thee!
    We never more may meet;
A sheer hulk I, nor e'er again
    Thy tiny form may greet.

In days, when far away at sea,
    In boyhood's early prime,
We met, and blythely fraternis'd,
    Nor cares were thine or mine.
Alas! the times are changed now,
    For I am old and grim;
And, should I thy great grandchild meet,
    I'd not be known by him.

Well, then, again, farewell to thee!
    When thou dost close thine eyes,
Thou hast not any more to do,
    Nor e'er again shalt rise.
But I, when earthly cares are o'er,
    Must enter life anew;
In hope's eternity shall prove
    As happy as 'tis true.

Tinto.

THE annexed lines were written for the purpose of being recited on Tinto on the occasion of a holiday excursion to the top of that celebrated mountain by the great number of men, in the service of James Ferguson, Esq., of Wiston, with their wives, children, and sweethearts, employed by him at his extensive gas coal works, at Auchinheath, Lanarkshire. The urbanity and kindness with which those people are uniformly treated by that gentleman are well known, and the consequence is, there is never any jarring between the parties, which so often disgraces works of a similar kind. Mr Ferguson having purchased the estate of Wiston, which stretches to the mountain's summit; and he, being in the habit of treating his people to an annual trip, and having gone to reside for a time on his new property, it was judiciously arranged that Tinto should be the locality visited on this occasion, 1870. The pleasures of the excursion were much enhanced by the generous hospitality with which the party were received at Wiston Lodge.

Tinto rises abruptly out of a table land on the west bank of the Clyde, not far from the source of that river. It is very steep on the south, east, and north sides, and slopes away to a moderate height to the westward. The east point, towering up to a considerable height, commands a very extensive view, as is attempted to be described in the verses. The west end is rent to the bottom by a remarkable chasm called "How Mouth." This most singular rend and a conical - shaped hill of considerable size, to the southward having something very peculiar about them, are said by tradition to have been the work of the wizard, Michael Scott, in company with an able, but very contumacious colleague, who are said to have executed many such vagaries in different parts of Scotland. Michael's head-quarters at the time were in the old Abbey of Glenluce in Galloway, where, it is gravely affirmed, his books still remain; but woe betide the wight who dare approach the vault containing them, as a shower of fire-balls issue forth on the approach of all intruders. Regarding the round hill in question, formed perhaps of the stuff taken from the gorge, which closely resembles a heap of sand after passing through a riddle, we are told that it was riddled in the common form by the worthy pair, alternately shovelling and using the riddle. And deponent sayeth that the wizard, while shovelling, pitched in an immense stone - yet to be seen at the foot of the hill - and injured the thumb of his worthy colleague, which irritated him so much that he threw down the sieve and "flew at Michael wi' furious ettle." The wizard instantly made tracks for Glenluce, right as the arrow flies, with his angry partner in his wake. Right in their line lay Cairntable hill, on the top of which the pursuer made a grab at the wizard, but at the moment tripped and fell, leaving the impression of his thighs and stern on the hill top, visible till this day. Michael profited by the fall, getting clear off. It may be doubted by some whether Michael's common ammunition of fire-balls would fend off such an opponent.

LINES TO BE RECITED ON TINTO.

Come, dear comrades, one and all,
  Fair or sable, short or tall,
On this our annual holiday,
  Set apart for harmless play,
Be as happy as we may.

Throw aside all care and sorrow,
On this lovely autumn morrow,
While from this fam'd mountain crown
Of Tinto, dress'd in purple gown,
We view the glorious prospect round.

See what fields of golden grain,
Garnish all the lowland plaid;
Look on Clyde's fantastic course,
Bursting from its humble source
Like silver thread on garment coarse.

See Lamington's old ruin grey,
And think on Marion Braidfoot's day,
The bride of Scotland's bravest chief,
Slain by a ruthless Southron thief,
Alas! her wedded joys were brief.

Look east toward the rising sun,
Where distant, Pentland, dark and dun,
Heaves up his form as if to hide,
"Auld Reekie" in her gaudy pride,
The mistress of the world wide.

Look far away to north and west,
Where huge Ben Lomond heaves his crest,
As if 'twas raised to prop the sky,
And bring the beauteous planets nigh,
To charm the wondering gazer's eye.

See round his base, like mirror spread,
To reproduce his lofty head,
The passing lovely Lomond lake
Winds gorgeously like glittering snake,
Emboss'd in copse and feathery brake.

Just where yon misty clouds arise,
The emporium of nations lies,
Where from each clime the world knows
The stately vessel comes and goes -
Glasgow, where commerce ebbs and flows.

And now, I ask one hearty cheer
   For generous friends who brought us here,
Whose unremitting kindness never
   Shall we forget - no, never, never!
And say, God bless them now and ever!

An Auld Man's Lament.

THRETTY thoosan' seven hunner an' auchty-five days
Ha'e pass't since my birthday 'mid the Galloway braes,
In an' auld reeky hoose on the brough o' Balfern -
An' nae doot I was coonted a verra fine bairn.
But the auld reekie hoose is nae mair tae be seen,
Baith the flure an' the yaird are noo glossy an' green,
An' the hare or the rabbit may cower on the hearth -
An' my dearest auld parents langsyne in the yearth.

That auld flure whaur my staucherin' fitsteps, nae doot,
Wad aye bring a' their love an' their tendernesss oot;
Whaur ilk e'enin', a psalm sung an' chapter was read,
An' a prayer sent tae heaven ere we lay doon in bed.
The whilk practice was guid, an' the gush o' the sang
Frae the auld reekie hoose, floatin' sweetly alang,
Wad astonish the folk o' these unco wise days,
Wha're sae little in love wi' their gran'father's ways.

Time crept on; we kept growin', my sister an' me,
Wi' the dear auld folk busy as busy could be;
We were sent tae the schule for a moothfu' o' lair -
Ah! we never could look for a bellyfu' there.
But it did weel eneuch, altho' no' muckle o't -
It aye sair't us tae coont a' the siller we got;
She gaed doon tae the grave wi' an unsullied fame,
An' it canna be lang till I follow her hame.

When I see the lov'd spot, saut tears fill my auld een,
Tae think what I was then, an' what since I ha'e been;
Hoo sae aft I hae swerved frae the coonsel then given,
Wi' their hearts fu' o' love tae direct me tae heaven;
I shall join them ere lang tae be pairted nae mair,
An' a hale host o' dear anes I hope to meet there;
What a privilege it is that the Christian can trust,
That he'll rise an' ascend amang those he loves most.

There's a new fangled race primed wi' wisdom an' speed,
Set aboot tae richt a' things by changin' oor creed;
But in time that's tae come, like the time that is gane,
Wi' th' auld Buke i' my oxter, I'se niffer wi' nane.
There is no muckle doot, that if I were tae prent
This short rhyme aboot byga'nes, by way of lament,
They wad say "There's a change; that is a' verra true
But it's no' in the times, frien' - it's only in you."

Weel-a-weel, I'se e'en drap it an' scribble nae langer -
It's no safe tae put they kin' o' folk in an anger;
I aye gat guid advice in the hamely auld ha';
An' I'se gang my ain gate - sae, guid day tae ye a'.
I ha'e rhym'd lang eneuch noo, a't fourscore an' four
I'll spoil nae mair Queen's English, it's time tae gi't owre
Sae I'll throw doon the pen, an' just claw my harnpan -
It was aye far owre thick for a sensible man.

The Sailor Boy's Log.

I'VE ceased to roam o'er the ocean's foam,
    And regained my native shore,
And here will I stay, nor again pass away,
    From the loved spot any more.
The tornado's full force I've met in it's course
    Of fire and thunder and rain,
When the eye was dim, from the lightning's gleam,
    And the thunder bellow'd amain.

I have tripped o'er the sand of the African strand,
    'Mong the naked sons of Ham;
Then far to the west, o'er the blue sea's crest,
    Crossed to pestilent Surinam.
There the crocodile grim, on the lagoon's brim,
    With his huge jaws opened wide,
To envelope the flies, while his gleaming eyes
    Kept watch on every side.

In the forest brake, that slimy snake,
    The boa-constrictor sly,
Through night and day lies in wait for its prey,
    That may heedless be passing by.
Let us flee while we've breath, from this region of death,
    That lurks under every tree;
Let us hie from the strand of this pestilent land,
    And cross the Atlantic sea.

An' island there stands, of all other lands,
    The glory and the pride is she;
The land of my birth, the sweetest on earth -
    Auld Scotland, Auld Scotland for me!
See her heathery hills and crystal rills,
    That descend from her mountains brown,
Where there's health on the gale, on mountain and vale,
    Joy and music in every sound.

The plover's lone wail sounds sad on the gale,
From the blaeberry bank on the moor;
While the cock's shrill cry wakes an echo nigh,
As he crows at the shepherd's door.
The innocent lamb, as it skips round its dam,
While she crops the flowery lea;
Each bleat that is given is a sound sent to heaven,
To tell how happy they be.

I'm safe moored at last from the hurricane's blast,
All my earthly wanderings done;
Contented I'll rest, waiting Heaven's behest.
When my numbered hours are run.

The Gloaming of a Spring Day.

ON an April eve, on the verge of May,
You are wandering lone, near the close of day,
On the western shore of old Caledon,
Where Atlantic waves break with heavy moan.
You stand in a vale, 'midst swelling hills,
Down whose slopes descend fertilising rills;
You look to the west, while a wimpling burn
Glides seaward with many a winding turn;
'Midst a scene like this the heart swells high,
With a balmy air and a cloudless sky.

You still look westward, when all other things
Are dwarf'd, blotted out, by the scene that springs;
As if taking to rest on the ocean's brim,
The great orb of day leans his lower limb;
He seems shorn of his beams, enlarged in size,
As if courting worship from human eyes.
And oh! what a glorious object is this,
Like an earthly gleam of heavenly bliss,
On the mighty waters seems newly spread
A golden carpet with diamonds o'erlaid.

You could gaze for ever, but our restless world,
By an unseen influence eastward hurl'd,
As a screen heaves up the glittering deep,
Sinks the glowing orb like a child to sleep;
As he sinks, and sinks, you gaze with delight,
While to you and the world he bids good night.
(The Connaught man says -'tis a shrewd remark -
He just descends to go back in the dark.)

You turn to go home, the ascent to climb,
Again you're spell-bound by the evening hymn,
All Nature speaks out with one voice to raise,
To the Power who feeds them, a song of praise.
The heatherbleat chicks and whirrs with his wing,
As he woos his mate by the sedgy spring;
The peesweep sweeps past with a peevish cry,
And the howlet hoots from the ruin nigh;
The cuckoo sounds her last note for the day,
And the heathcock's hoarse crow winds up the lay
'Tis harmony from discordant sound,
And tells the joy of creation round.

Aroused by the silence, you raise your eyes,
To the coming glory of evening skies;
The stars come out bright, as if one by one,
Like angels' sweet eyes looking down on man;
You hie to your cot on the upland lea,
Shelter'd well by a bouzie bourtrie tree;
A gloaming like this is a sermon given,
To smooth our rough path on our way to heaven.

On the Loss of the Monarch.

LINES written at the request of the lady of Captain Kirkcaldy, of the emigrant ship *Monarch*, which sailed from Liverpool to New York in March, 1866, with 800 passengers and 57 of a crew and was never again heard of:-

> The ways of that dread power that governs man
> Are oft mysterious - impossible to scan!
> We see the good and prized so oft cut down,
> While wicked men are prospering all around -
> We see the best and bravest of mankind
> Laid low, while knaves and fools are left behind -
> We see the brave and generous swept away,
> The loved and valued drop from day to day,
> By treach'ry, murdered, or in battle slain,
> Or meet their fate upon the boisterous main:
> One melancholy tale of modern date
> Stands out to tell of such a direful fate.

> From Liverpool the good ship *Monarch* bore
> With emigrants for old Columbia's shore -
> Beloved Kirkcaldy, captain - seaman true
> As ever crossed the mighty waters blue.
> Eight hundred passengers were all well told.
> With fifty-seven true British seamen bold,
> Alas! no ear e'er heard, no tongue can tell
> What sad catastrophe to them befell!
> Engulph'd by storm, they found a watery grave
> To sleep uncoffined 'neath the roaring wave!
> And gallant Reid, a youth of promise high,
> In blooming manhood also doomed to die
> Let us beware of censuring God's great cause
> Who governs by general, not by partial laws;
> He takes his own away from ills foreseen,

To heavenly palaces 'mid pastures green:
While wicked men, who have their portion here,
Are left to run their infamous career.

To those who mourn the loss of dear ones gone,
A loving husband, or a darling son,
Who find the dear ones from their bosom riven
To 'scape a coming ill are snatched to heaven -
Look up to Him who hears the widow's moan
At midnight hour, when by herself alone;
Or cherishing a pledge of mutual love
Whose sire's an angel in the realms above -
Rejoicing in the coming realms when they
Shall join him in that land of endless day!
Let those who mourn look upward, onward still,
Nor brood too deeply on a bygone ill;
In time they'll find 'twas "blessing in disguise,"
When the loved one was carried to the skies;
'Twill tend to soften down their heavy grief,
And bring their yearning bosoms much relief.

Oh! thou Great Power, whose sweetest name is "Love,"
Who govern'st all below and all above,
Strengthen the widow's heart, let grace preside,
Soften her sorrows and her footsteps guide!
Her "Olive Plant," Oh! nourish, lead, defend,
Through life's short journey to a blessed end!
That all may join, when earthly cares are o'er,
No more to part, to grieve - no, never more!

Farewell to Galloway.

"Breathes there the man with soul so dead,
Who never to himself hath said,
This is my own my native land!
Whose heart hath ne'er within him burned,
As home his footsteps he hath turned
From wand'ring on a foreign strand!"

                                    - Sir W . Scott.

IF this is so, surely the hallow'd space
Which first he saw deserves the highest place;
And should he wander many a weary day,
And when returned he finds all swept away -
The friends and comrades of his early hours
Not to be found among their former bowers;
Tis sad again to leave, but go he must -
There's no communion ev'n with kindred dust.
Ah! what a wondrous change is wrought by time
Since first he left to visit foreign clime;
A sick'ning change - he cannot linger here,
The charm has vanish'd made the spot so dear.
Had he ne'er left thy lovely little hills,
Sweet Galloway, fumed for bubbling crystal rills,
Thou would'st have still retained his virgin love,
As then no rival could his fancy move;
But viewing other lands has dwarf'd thy looks -
Thy mountains sunk to hills, thy rivers brooks;
Had he ne'er seen the mighty Amazon,
Or towering Teneriffe in burning zone,
He would have thought that nowhere else could be
Rivers and hills that could compete with thee.
Such is my case, I far away must hie,
And seek a place to lay me down and die;
To thee, sweet spot, I now must bid adieu,

For never more shall I revisit you;
No son of thine at any former time,
That ever left thee for a foreign clime,
Ador'd thee with a love surpassing mine.
The last of all my race - 'tis hard to leave,
Nor lay my bones within my father's grave.
But truce with this! What matter where the spot
Where this old carcase must lie down and rot;
A glorious fabric that shall ne'er decay
Shall join the spirit on a future day;
A hope so cheering ought to float me o'er
Life's stormy billows to a happy shore.
When I look back to boyhood's early prime,
When all was sunshine, and no cares were mine,
When bustling 'mong my schoolmates on the lea -
Of whom not one blythe face remains to see -
All, all have crossed that so much dreaded bourne,
From whence no fugitive shall e'er return!
A solemn thought for me, that I alone
Am ling'ring here when all the rest are gone;
It seems so strange than on my native shore
Kindred or schoolmate I shall meet no more.
But I'll look back once more - I'll not complain,
I'll summon up my early friends again,
A period yet untouched remains to scan
Of vast importance to the coming man,
When love, the most refining power below,
Warms his young bosom with a generous glow;
The sun shines brighter - all he sees and hears
Are sweeter far than ought of bygone years;
As if transported to a sunnier clime,
The youth feels manhood come before its time.
The softening influence of such a flame
Awakes new thoughts for which he has no name -
A wish to shine, to gain the just esteem
Of her he loves, the sweetener of his dream!
So dear he loves her, he would condescend
To call her household dog a kindly friend;
Yea, even the smoke from her loved cot that comes
Curls far more graceful than from other lums -

'Tis generous love refines and smoothes him down:
The youth who never loved remains a clown.
But truce again - I hasten to a close,
This silly rhyme that's neither verse nor prose;
Yet, in my homespun way I fain would tell
I still have Galloway friends whom I love well,
Descendants of my mates in days of yore,
That show me kindness, like their sires before;
I can't express the thanks I fain would speak -
The spirit's willing, but the talent's weak.

The River Bladenoch.

THE fine little river Bladenoch issues from a sheet of water on the marches of the shires of Ayr and Wigton, in Galloway, called Loch Maberry, of about three-fourths of a mile in length and one-fourth broad. Its margins and surroundings are bleak and lonely; bent and heather the only vegetation on its banks or vicinity. Following its windings down to Wigton Bay into which it falls, on the south side of the town, where it forms a harbour; the length of the run may be about fifteen miles. It is navigable only for about a short mile, at the fine old tower of Baldoon, the navigable portion passing through low land reclaimed from the sea. On its start it runs due south over a bed of round whinstone boulders, and the descent being considerable it dashes along very rapidly. For a considerable way from its source it is a small stream with banks as tame and naked as possible. It divides the parishes of Penningham and Kirkcowan for some miles, and Wigton and Kirkinner lower down. East of Kirkcowan village it is joined by the water of Tarff, and a few miles farther down by another burn, when it wheels due east and continues so to the sea. Its banks, throughout the eastward portion of its course through a rich and well cultivated strath, are very fine, adorned with clumps of beautiful old trees, whilst it drives several mills in its progress. About two miles from the sea it is turned south for a short distance through a narrow gorge between two high hills, wooded to their summits, - the finest scenery of its whole run. The descent here is steep, over a bed of rugged rock, when it settles in the large pool of Linghoor, one of the finest salmon pools in Scotland. From this point to the bay it runs east, passing a new and old bridge of two large arches, and the ancient tower of Baldoon, its course almost level and banks very grand. Formerly when joining the sea it swept away north round the hill on which Wigton stands, joining the river Cree at low water about two miles down the bay. I know well the following lines are a tame affair;but they may tempt some one else to do the sweet little river more credit by singing its praise more in accordance with its merits. I am not aware that any one ever before attempted to rhyme it into notice.

LINES ON THE RIVER BLADENOCH.

From Maberry's loch, in a region drear,
The Bladenoch starts on his seaward career;
Not a tree bathes its roots in his crystal stream,
Nor throws its shadow o'er the region grim.
'Tis silence all - not a sound strikes the ear,
Save the curlew's wail as he passes near;
Or the lapwing's peevish and angry cry,
While guarding her young on the bent hard by.
O'er a bed of boulders he tumbles along,
The bubbling spray singing cheerful song;
His course is brief, and he must not stay,
Till he joins with the lovely Wigton bay.
From the west old Tarff comes thundering down,
And their streams unite due east from Kirkcowan;
Augmented he wheels round many a turn,
And is joined anon by Culmaze burn.
On his banks as he passes ancient Grange, -
He now looks east, - what a magical change!
'Tis autumn, and patches of golden hue
Enrich his course - 'tis beautiful now.
But what shall we say of old Torehouse shore,
Where King Galdus was slain in days of yore,
And the Druids tumuli, which, till this day,
Still shew, as of old, their circle grey.
Huge granite boulders, like ghosts on the moor,

Where brownies and fairies hold annual splore,
Old Bladenoch, nam'd from King Galdus slain,
Hurries speedily past the insanguin'd plain.

A rend in the hills allows him to pour
His waters to rest in far fam'd Linghoor;
After such a long and rugged race,
'Tis pleasant to find such a resting place.
Refresh'd like a giant after his wine,
Old Bladenoch moves slowly 'twixt banks divine,
Passing under two bridges, old and new,
Till Baldoon's old tower comes into view.
But hark! did you hear that piercing cry
From yon old grey tower in the wood hard by?
'Twas so wild and fiendish, so shrill and loud,
As to ring on the sky through the riven cloud!
We pause for a time, a murmur we hear
From the frighten'd fugitives passing near,
That the bride of Dunbar had mangl'd her groom
In their bridal chamber in midnight gloom.
By sore unrelenting cruelty driven,
To forfeit a pledge of true love given,
She drew a dagger and stabb'd her lord,
Then pierc'd her own heart on the chamber board;
The fam'd wizard's hand who gave us the lore,
Wove the tale into "Bride of Lammermoor."

Once more we must follow the river's way,
To the passing lovely Wigton bay,
Where once in his stream by a cruel band,
Bound fast to stakes by their command,
Two heroic females, whom God had bless'd,
Were "chas'd up to Heaven," for ever to rest.
On that tragic spot the cattle now graze,
As old Bladenoch has fled in great amaze:
Cut out a new course far down in the sand,
And left in a fright the murd'rous strand.
Few rivers in Scotland can furnish a claim
To more notice in history than Bladenoch stream.

The Nethan Water.

THE course of this stream - from its origin, on the east side of the Cummerhead hills, until it is lost in the Clyde at Crossford - is entirely confined to the parish of Lesmahagow, and is through a valley extremely beautiful and picturesque. Few rural streams of equal dimensions can cope with it in respect of the natural grandeur, as well as the artificial adornment of its banks, there being six magnificent villas standing almost at equal distances along its whole length, finishing with Craignethan Castle, the immortal "Tillietudlem" of the great novelist. Almost at its very source stands the house of Stockbriggs, the residence of the Alston family, surrounded by thriving plantations, the delightful green slopes, and fertile fields - lately brown heathery barren braes - of the upland portion of the estate hearing ample evidence of the untiring enterprise of the late J. W. Alston, Esq. It is here joined by the Logan water, not the Logan referred to in the mournful plaint of the disconsolate maiden -

> "Nae mair at Logan Kirk will he,
> Atween the preachings, meet wi' me,
> Meet wi' me; and, when it's mirk,
> Convoy me hame frae Logan Kirk."

The stream, thus augmented, flows through the equally well wooded grounds of Auchlochan, the property of J. T. Brown, Esq. - a cozie-looking hall peeping out, the very picture of ease, peace, and comfort. By a graceful bend, it turns due north to Trows, the property of R. M'Ghie, Esq., and soon sweeps past the mansion of Birkwood, a modern structure of great beauty, with two lofty castellated towers, the residence of J. G. M'Kirdy, Esq., which, from position and surroundings, is the most picturesque of the whole. The valley now assumes a more romantic character - high, steep heavily-wooded banks on the east side, and church, manse, and glebe, holm patches, and village of Abbeygreen on the west, till it passes the venerable mansion-house of Auchtyfardle, lately modernised by the proprietor, Major Mosman. Throughout the whole of Auchtyfardle grounds the banks are very rich in varied beauty. A little onward the stream passes Kerse House, the property of J. B. Greenshields, Esq., situated on a beautiful terrace among stupendous trees on its western bank. It is a fine specimen of the Elizabethan order, built a few years ago, and finished in a style that renders it one of the most comfortable residences in the country. Downwards still, the most romantic portion of its course is reached at Auchinheath, where it enters an immense gorge, apparently the result of some convulsion of nature, as if to form an outlet for the accumulated waters of the uplands, the banks high and ruggedly precipitous on both sides. On the top of the east bank, with a magnificent aspect to south, west, and north, stands the unique cottage of James Ferguson, Esq., a thing that must have occurred to the mind of the talented and tasteful gentleman (as he is his own architect) some night when ''a dream stood at his head;'' and it would seem as if, when he awoke, Alladin had lent him a rub of his ''old lamp,'' and up rose the image of his dream in this remarkable structure. Equally original and refined taste is displayed in the fantastic web of walks and other efforts to add to the beauties of nature on the face of the precipice descending to the water. A little further down, the gorge is spanned by a railway bridge of great height and lightness of construction, and soon the direct course of the stream is opposed by a steep bank, which sends it due north, coasting the lovely holm of

"Tillietudlem," the expulsion from which so sorely afflicted the heart of poor "Cuddy Headrigg" - evidently not a very sensitive one - especially, as he was not sure if he could turn a furrow anywhere else. Had the course of the Nethan hitherto been of the most tame and unattractive nature, the fact that here it washes the foot of that romantic rock on which stands Craignethan Castle, would alone be sufficient to raise it to a renown equal to that of Tweed or Yarrow. "Tillietudlem" - where Queen Mary slept the night before the battle of Langside - where King Charles breakfasted, to the inexpressible delight of old Lady Bellenden - where "bloody Clavers" shewed his iron will and unfeeling heart - and where poor "Cuddy" was so Wantonly treated by Jenny Dennison, his joe - is no common pile of stone and lime. Not being qualified to add one single shade to its fame, we "leave it alone in its glory". The remarkable rend in the rocky bank, to allow the Nethan to join the Clyde, a little further down, is one of the most singular features in its whole course. The following lines will, no doubt, appear to some minds so very tame as to pay but a poor compliment to this romantic little stream; and the thought may be suggested that it might have been better to leave it too "alone in its glory" than to send its praises abroad, hobbling on crutches:-

LINES TO THE NETHAN.

No poet, in his dream, has had Nethan for his theme,
    Nor sounded his praise in a song;
Yet, not the less, his praise deserves the richest lays,
    As he gracefully sweeps along.
His course is quickly run - ended ere well begun -
    Yet, on his wooded banks around
From Cummer to the Clyde, rich gems on every side
    Of both art and nature abound.
From 'mong heather and gall, near Stockbriggs Gothic hall,
    He starts on his winding career,

Soon join'd by Logan's flood, sweeps through Auchlochan wood,
  As he bounds along bright and clear.
Passing Birkwood's lofty tower, 'mong bonny woods and flowers,
  He enters consecrated ground,
Where St. Machute's monks told beads, and mumbled Popish
      creeds,
  While old Nethan murmur'd around.
Ah! those were happy times, when rung the vesper chimes,
  And a monk kept the conscience clear,
When, for every sin and shame that the tongue of man could name,
  Forgiveness could be purchas'd here!
To follow Nethan down, and leave this holy ground,
  Passing Aughty's stately old halls,
Sometimes o'er tiny linn he leaps with little din,
  And sometimes listlessly crawls.
See Kerse so lovely stand, 'mid trees on terrace grand,
  Enriching the western side;
Old Nethan's spirits rise as on and on he flies,
  Like the rush of a high spring-tide.
What gorge is this ahead, by ancient earthquake made,
  With a gem on its shoulder high -
The wonder of the time, "a romance in stone and lime,"
  A work of skilful hand and eye?
More rapid on his path, he tumbles down the strath,
  Beneath a mimic rainbow span,
Quite a gossamer affair, suspended in mid air,
  By the wonderful skill of man.
On classic ground once more, the pridle of Nethan's shore,
  To old Tillietudlem all hail!
Ah! the wizard hand is cold, the bewitching tale that told.
  Wail! Scotland, auld Scotland, wail!
Pause! dear old Nethan, pause! don't rush into the jaws
  Of that huge glen gaping wide!
Thou wont! - then, fare-thee-well! thy byegone tale I'll tell
  Since thou'rt left me, and married to the Clyde.

Address to the Moon on New-Year's Eve
1872.

TAK' yer time, auld moon, why lea' us sae soon
    By hilchin' roun' yer cauldrife side!
Ye're changefu', nae doot, but come shining oot
    Tae regulate oor time an' tide.
Wise sages can tell exceedingly well
    Of yer history past and tae run,
Of yer power sae rare o'er oor atmosphere,
    An' yer league wi' the blazing sun.

An' they also can tell, as true an' as well,
    Of yer power o'er the human brain,
How its moods ye can change, soothe down, or derange,
    In yer course as ye wax and wane.
Wha hasna seen, on a village green,
    Where an idiot chanced to remain,
The wonderfu' power of thy changin' hour
    On the madden'd maniac's brain?

Some doctors, 'tis true, tell us this will not do;
    But when such an assertion was made,
There can be nae doot ye were shinin' oot
    Full an' roon as the doctor's head.
O! 'twas surely gran', your first glimpse o' man
    In Eden wi' his bonnie bride -
In the gloamin' hour, near his bridal bower,
    'Mang flower by the river side!

Ay, 'twas lang, lang syne, but ye'll mind it fine,
    Though five thoosan' year hae sped,
Yet ye're beamin' as bricht as ye did that nicht
    When shinin' on their marriage bed.
Frae that time till this no such earthly bliss

Hae ye witness'd without alloy,
Nor for time tae come, till the day of doom,
Shall ye look on unmingled joy.
'Twere ower lang tae tell of the wonderfu' spell
Ye hold over earth, air, an' sea,
An' language wad fail tae tell the hale tale
Of thy magic an' glamourie.

Lines on the Marriage of Lord Earlies.

A JOYOUS sound from Galloway,
Boding good for the coming day,
Telling the noble Stewart has led
A Cecil to his marriage bed;
With them may grace divine abide,
And offspring bliss their fireside!
Such unions of the good and great
Form bulwarks for the Church and State;
The spinal marrow of our isle,
Safe guardians over those who toil;
And while such influence rules the hour,
Let maniacs rave for lawless power.
Stand forth, then, all who dare be free,
From Patrick's Port to Brig of Cree,
From Galloway Mull to Corswall stran',
Support your noble Member's plan,
Hold fast what long experience tell,
What common sense confirms as well -
That those whom God's own charter guides
Are truly free, and none besides.
Let giddy men hunt phantoms wild,
By reckless demagogues beguiled;
Stand fast, and stem the coming storm,
Grossly mis-named a just reform.
February 7th, 1872.

In Memory of a Beloved Wife.

SHE'S gone from me, the nearest
    Of all my earthly kin,
She whom my soul loved dearest,
    While in this world of sin.

That holy band is riven -
    To us a silken tie -
And she is gone to heaven -
    Left me alone to sigh.

No language yet invented
    Can tell of all my love -
How much I have lamented
    Since she has gone above.

Father! I know 'tis sinful
    Thy high behest to scorn;
But when the eye is brimful,
    The stricken heart will mourn.

Surely that soothing weakness
    Finds pardon in the end,
When He whose soul was meekness
    Wept for a common friend.

Sweet saint! thou cannot hear me
    When I make heavy moan,
But I will soon be near thee,
    My time must soon be gone.

Then what a joyful greeting
    Upon that blessed shore;
Our last and sweetest meeting -
    To meet to part no more.

On Bladenoch's banks in sadness
I lately roam'd, where we
Oft met in joy and gladness
At the dear old trysting tree.

But all was dark and cheerless,
No wonted form was there;
That form so sweet and peerless
Is gone for ever mair.

FINIS.

Book List 1996

G.C. BOOK PUBLISHERS LTD

SHOP, OFFICE & GALLERY
17 NORTH MAIN STREET
WIGTOWN
DUMFRIES & GALLOWAY, SCOTLAND

Open Mon - Sat   9.00am to 5pm

All of the items in this list may be obtained by mail order or by visiting our Book Shop in Wigtown. Postage is extra, please add £1.50 for UK delivery.

The Book Shop stocks nearly 40,000 books, new and secondhand. There are five rooms, one of which is devoted to Scottish books, a second room is used as a gallery where antiques, pictures and books on the arts are displayed.

Free coffee is served all day.

Terms: CASH WITH ORDER. IF OVERSEAS WE WILL ACCEPT AN INTERNATIONAL MONEY ORDER or BANKERS DRAFT IN STERLING.
VISA & MASTERCARDS ACCEPTED

FOR FURTHER READING

"Wigtown Ploughman" by John MacNeillie. This powerful novel set at the turn of the century in Wigtownshire caused a stir when it was first published in 1938. It portrayed life on the land for the ordinary working man in its true light, much to the chagrin of the middle classes who would have preferred leaving it unacknowledged. This was his second novel. He has now written over 45 mostly under his gaelic name of "Ian Niall".
ISBN 1/872350/10/0   £4.95

"The Scottish Music Hall 1850 - 1990". by Jimmy Littlejohn. This book is an extremely comprehensive work of reference apart from being a good read, it contains photos, playbills and programmes of times gone by in the theatres of Glasgow, Edinburgh and most other places in Scotland.
ISBN 1/872350/05/4   £7.95

"The Birds In Wigtownshire" by R. C. Dickson. An invaluable work of reference never before available. Contains bird lists, statistics, and photographs of species and habitat. A serious contribution to the study of ornithology.
ISBN 1/872350/35/6   £6.95

"Scotland's Native Horse, its history, breeding and survival" by Robert Beck. The definitive work on the survival of the native horse in the form of the ponies of Eriskay in the Outer Hebrides. Contains graphs, drawings, diagrams and photographs. The sum total of 20 years work by well known Scottish vet.
ISBN 1/872350/25/9   £7.95

"Highways and Byways in Galloway and Carrick" by Rev. Dick. This book is a limited edition reprint of the first edition published in 1916. It has the same blue cover and comes with a redesigned dust jacket with an original Hugh Thomas illustration. This book is in great demand as an out of print book.
ISBN 1/872350/55/0   £14.95

"High Endeavours" Experiences of members of the West Riding Branch of the Aircrew Association. Nearly 50 previously unpublished stories of humour, heroism, valour and stoicism in the face of overwhelming odds. 270 pages text, cartoonsand log book entries. Laminated hard-back covers in full colour.
ISBN 1/872350/11/9   £14.95

"The Great Ingratitude - Bomber Command in World War II" by James Fyfe. An appreciation of the sacrifice made by members of Bomber Commandin World War II. This book is in answer to the ill informed criticism of the role played by "Bomber" Harris and his crews in stemming the tide of Hitler's ambitions in Europe.
ISBN 1/872350/75/5   £16.95

"Second Daughter" by Donna Brewster. A historical novel of the "killing times" in Galloway during the period of the struggle of the Covenanters. Based on fact and five years research by the author.
ISBN 0/948278/13/7   £3.75

"Survival Was For Me" by Duncan Wilson. An ordinary soldier in the British Army tells of his experiences at the Fall of Singapore and afterwards as a prisoner of the Japanese in Malaya and Thailand.
ISBN 1/872350/20/8   £6.45

"Persecutions in Scotland 1603 -1685". Explanatory booklet designed to help the reader understand the conflicts betweenthe Church and the people during the 18th century and how it led to the establishment of the Covenanters in Scottish history.
ISBN 1/872350/36/4   £4.00

"The Public Roads and Bridges in Dumfriesshire 1650 - 1820" by James Robertson former County Surveyor. A comprehensive history of the development of the road system in the county from the earliest times, through the Roman period down to the improvements of the 18th and 19th centuries. Many hundreds of verbatim minute records relating to the building of the bridges and the setting up of the toll roads. Comes complete with a full colour map published in 1807 based on Crawford's survey of 1804.
ISBN 1/872350/65/8   £12.95

"Ruby" by Sarah McFarlane Wylie. An eye witness account of life in the early 20th century in Glasgow and Galloway. Mrs Wylie has recorded her childhood with great clarity. This book is an important record of social life linking industrial Glasgow with the rural heartland of Galloway
ISBN 1/872350/45/3   £2.95

"The Lonsdale Battalion" by Colin Bardgett. A comprehensive work of reference relating to the raising of Lord Lonsdale's battalion for service with Kitchener's Army in France and Flanders during the First World War. The book contains eyewitness accounts, a complete list of casualties, awards for gallantry and many previously unpublished photographs of the young men who made up the battalion. Comes with a full colour reproduction (half size) of the infamous "Man or Mouse" poster.
ISBN 1/872350/60/7   £14.95

"The History of the Lands and their Owners in Galloway" by Peter H M'Kerlie. This is a facsimile of M'Kerlie's own copy of this very important work. It contains many additions and corrections in his own handwriting. Quarter bound in red and black cloth, over 2500 pp and nearly 100 drawings executed by M'Kerlie himself.   Limited edition of 350 sets only.
ISBN 1/872350/90/9   5 Volumes   £100.00